D1710666

Ancient Greece

Other titles in the series include:

Ancient Egypt
Ancient Rome
The Black Death
The Decade of the 2000s
The Holocaust
The Early Middle Ages
The Late Middle Ages
The Renaissance

Ancient Greece

Hal Marcovitz

Bruno Leone
Series Consultant

San Diego, CA

Printed in the United States

For more information, contact:
ReferencePoint Press, Inc.
PO Box 27779
San Diego, CA 92198
www.ReferencePointPress.com

LIBRARY OF CONGRESS CATALOGING-IN-PUBLICATION DATA

Marcovitz, Hal.
Ancient Greece / by Hal Marcovitz.
p. cm. -- (Understanding world history series)
Includes bibliographical references and index.
ISBN 978-1-60152-284-9 (hardback) -- ISBN 1-60152-284-3 (hardback) 1. Greece--Civilization--To 146 B.C.--Juvenile literature. I. Title.
DF77.M297 2012
938--dc23
2011048991

Contents

Foreword 6

Important Events in Ancient Greece 8

Introduction 10
The Defining Characteristics of Ancient Greece

Chapter One 15
What Conditions Led to the Rise of Ancient Greece?

Chapter Two 29
Rise of the City-States

Chapter Three 42
An Era of Achievement

Chapter Four 55
The Decline and Fall of Ancient Greece

Chapter Five 68
What Is the Legacy of Ancient Greece?

Source Notes 81

Important People of Ancient Greece 84

For Further Research 87

Index 90

Picture Credits 95

About the Author 96

Foreword

When the Puritans first emigrated from England to America in 1630, they believed that their journey was blessed by a covenant between themselves and God. By the terms of that covenant they agreed to establish a community in the New World dedicated to what they believed was the true Christian faith. God, in turn, would reward their fidelity by making certain that they and their descendants would always experience his protection and enjoy material prosperity. Moreover, the Lord guaranteed that their land would be seen as a shining beacon—or in their words, a "city upon a hill,"—which the rest of the world would view with admiration and respect. By embracing this notion that God could and would shower his favor and special blessings upon them, the Puritans were adopting the providential philosophy of history—meaning that history is the unfolding of a plan established or guided by a higher intelligence.

The concept of intercession by a divine power is only one of many explanations of the driving forces of world history. Historians and philosophers alike have subscribed to numerous other ideas. For example, the ancient Greeks and Romans argued that history is cyclical. Nations and civilizations, according to these ancients of the Western world, rise and fall in unpredictable cycles; the only certainty is that these cycles will persist throughout an endless future. The German historian Oswald Spengler (1880–1936) echoed the ancients to some degree in his controversial study *The Decline of the West.* Spengler asserted that all civilizations inevitably pass through stages comparable to the life span of a person: childhood, youth, adulthood, old age, and, eventually, death. As the title of his work implies, Western civilization is currently entering its final stage.

Joining those who see purpose and direction in history are thinkers who completely reject the idea of meaning or certainty. Rather, they reason that since there are far too many random and unseen factors at work on the earth, historians would be unwise to endorse historical predictability of any type. Warfare (both nuclear and conventional), plagues, earthquakes, tsunamis, meteor showers, and other catastrophic world-changing events have loomed large throughout history and prehistory. In his essay "A Free Man's Worship," philosopher and mathematician Bertrand Russell (1872–1970) supported this argument, which many refer to as the nihilist or chaos theory of history. According to Russell, history follows no preordained path. Rather, the earth itself and all life on earth resulted from, as Russell describes it, an "accidental collocation of atoms." Based on this premise, he pessimistically concluded that all human achievement will eventually be "buried beneath the debris of a universe in ruins."

Whether history does or does not have an underlying purpose, historians, journalists, and countless others have nonetheless left behind a record of human activity tracing back nearly 6,000 years. From the dawn of the great ancient Near Eastern civilizations of Mesopotamia and Egypt to the modern economic and military behemoths China and the United States, humanity's deeds and misdeeds have been and continue to be monitored and recorded. The distinguished British scholar Arnold Toynbee (1889–1975), in his widely acclaimed 12-volume work entitled *A Study of History,* studied 21 different civilizations that have passed through history's pages. He noted with certainty that others would follow.

In the final analysis, the academic and journalistic worlds mostly regard history as a record and explanation of past events. From a more practical perspective, history represents a sequence of building blocks—cultural, technological, military, and political—ready to be utilized and enhanced or maligned and perverted by the present. What that means is that all societies—whether advanced civilizations or preliterate tribal cultures—leave a legacy for succeeding generations to either embrace or disregard.

Recognizing the richness and fullness of history, the ReferencePoint Press Understanding World History series fosters an evaluation and interpretation of history and its influence on later generations. Each volume in the series approaches its subject chronologically and topically, with specific focus on nations, periods, or pivotal events. Primary and secondary source quotations are included, along with complete source notes and suggestions for further research.

Moreover, the series reflects the truism that the key to understanding the present frequently lies in the past. With that in mind, each series title concludes with a legacy chapter that highlights the bonds between past and present and, more important, demonstrates that world history is a continuum of peoples and ideas, sometimes hidden but there nonetheless, waiting to be discovered by those who choose to look.

Important Events in Ancient Greece

4000 BC
Civilization emerges in Greece as migrants settle there during the final years of the Stone Age.

1300 BC
Settlers establish a community at Athens, which will grow into one of ancient Greece's most powerful city-states and later the capital of modern Greece.

1250 BC
A Greek army sacks the city of Troy, bringing to a close the 10-year Trojan War.

1100 BC
The Dorians invade Greece from the north, establishing a settlement at Corinth and later a settlement at what would become Sparta, one of ancient Greece's most powerful city-states.

ca. 800 BC
Homer writes the poems the *Iliad* and the *Odyssey,* giving a mythical version of the siege of Troy as well as other events in the lives of Greek heroes.

776 BC
The first Olympic Games are staged near the city of Olympia. Athletes from across Greece compete in the games before as many as 50,000 spectators.

594 BC
The aristocrat Solon becomes ruler of Athens. As part of his rule, he recognizes the rights of ordinary citizens, wiping out their debts and freeing many from slavery.

508 BC
Athenians overthrow the dictator Isagoras and invite the exiled aristocrat Cleisthenes to lead the city-state. Cleisthenes establishes the Athenian Assembly, the first democratic body of lawmakers in history.

490 BC
At the Battle of Marathon, the outnumbered Athenians defeat an invading force of Persians during the first Greco-Persian War.

4000 / 1400 1100 800 500

405 BC
Athens loses the naval battle of Aegospotamoi; its fleet wiped out, Athens has now lost the ability to continue the war.

399 BC
The philosopher Socrates is made a scapegoat for the Athenian loss in the Peloponnesian War; he is tried on trumped up charges of worshipping false gods and corrupting youth, found guilty, and executed.

336 BC
Alexander the Great, a Macedonian prince, unites all Greek armies under his command. Alexander's empire falls in 323 BC shortly after his death.

480 BC
During the second Greco-Persian War, a fighting force of 300 Spartans and 700 allies from Thespiae hold off tens of thousands of Persian invaders for three days at the Battle of Thermopylae before a Greek traitor betrays the defenders, leading to their slaughter.

470 430 390 350 310 / 150

404 BC
Athens surrenders to Sparta, ending the Peloponnesian War.

146 BC
Rome completes its conquest of the Greek city-states, bringing the entire country under its domination. Greece remains under Roman rule until the Roman Empire collapses 500 years later.

431 BC
A dispute between the colony Corcyra and the city-state Corinth expands into a civil war that involves all city-states in Greece. Athens and Sparta become the primary combatants in the Peloponnesian War.

413 BC
A two-year campaign by Athenian soldiers on the island of Sicily ends in defeat; all Athenians are slaughtered by the Spartan warriors.

478 BC
The city-states of Greece form the Delian League to protect themselves against future Persian invasions. The league protects Greece for nearly 50 years, but eventually disputes and jealousies among members cause the downfall of the league.

Introduction

The Defining Characteristics of Ancient Greece

To have been a citizen of ancient Greece was to have lived in a very dynamic period of history. The ancient Greeks made many important discoveries in science, mathematics, and medicine. They erected some of the most impressive buildings in the ancient world and blazed new trails in art as well as literature and ceramics. The Greeks founded philosophy—raising questions about the nature of human thought and conduct. They invented competitive sports. Indeed, the word "stadium" has its origin in the Greek language.

The era of dominance by the ancient Greeks lasted some 1,100 years. It started with the Greek victory in the Trojan War in about 1250 BC and lasted until 146 BC when the Greeks were conquered by the Romans. During their era of power, influence, and scholarship the Greeks established principles that still guide people and institutions today. Says historian Michael Grant of Cambridge University in England, "The ancient Greeks are so significant that they demand to be studied in their own right, and not merely as forerunners of ourselves. Yet at the same time, different though many of their circumstances and problems inevitably must have been, they *were* our forerunners, the ancestors and sources of our own western civilization—for better or worse."[1]

Remarkably, perhaps, all of these accomplishments occurred in a country marked by disunity. Greece was dominated by many city-states. Originally small settlements of migrants from other portions of

Europe or from Asia and North Africa, some of these city-states grew into powerful domains that boasted rich treasuries and fearsome armies and navies. During the era of ancient Greece, the two most dominant city-states were Athens and Sparta.

Athens and Sparta

A male citizen of Athens held a special place in the ancient world. By the sixth century BC, whether he was a wealthy aristocrat, farmer, craftsman or lowly laborer, the Athenian had the right to stand up in an assembly and voice his opinion about the direction of his government. Moreover, he had the right to vote on issues debated in the assembly and everyone's vote was equal—the vote of the aristocrat in the Athenian Assembly was considered equal to the vote of the laborer or craftsman. Some 1,700 years before the Magna Carta limited the authority of the monarchy in England, and 2,300 years before the drafting of the US Constitution, the Athenians had conceived the earliest form of democracy.

West of Athens, in the Greek city-state of Sparta, life was much different. The Spartans remained under the authority of a king—there was no democracy in Sparta. Moreover, the Spartan male was raised to be a warrior. From the earliest age he was schooled in the art of combat and expected to follow his commander into battle with unquestioned loyalty. Says historian Will Durant,

> The power and pride of Sparta was above all in its army, for in the courage, discipline, and skill of these troops it found its security and its ideal. Every citizen was trained for war, and was liable for military service from his twentieth to sixtieth year.
>
> Around this army Sparta formed its moral code: to be good was to be strong and brave; to die in battle was the highest honor and happiness; to survive defeat was a disgrace that even the soldier's mother could hardly forgive. "Return with your shield or on it," was the Spartan mother's farewell to her soldier son.[2]

Women, Slaves, and War

Women in Athens, Sparta, and other city-states enjoyed the fruits of their societies, but they held far fewer rights than the male citizens. In aristocratic homes, special rooms—usually on the second floor—were reserved for female occupation. After their marriages, the principal responsibilities of Greek women were to bear and care for the children, weave fabric, and maintain the household. Says historian Colette Hemingway,

> The culmination of a young woman's socialization was her marriage, which usually took place at the age of fourteen or fifteen. Marriage did not require a young bride's consent, as she was simply passed from the protection of her father to that of her husband. A young woman in classical Athens lacked any rights of citizenship, and could only be described as the wife of an Athenian citizen.[3]

Even worse off were the slaves, who were bought and sold in the agoras, the Greek marketplaces, alongside the grapes, olives, and figs. Slaves were typically soldiers captured in war or citizens of conquered lands. Some worked in the households of the aristocracy; others were forced into hard labor in the mines that produced the metals for the swords and armor of the Greek armies.

Throughout the ancient era there were other city-states in Greece, but Athens and Sparta dominated life, politics, and the culture of the country. And for much of the ancient era, Athens and Sparta were rivals—over the centuries the two city-states maintained an uneasy peace. They distrusted one another and would eventually fight a long and devastating war that would help spark the decline of Greece as a power in the Mediterranean and lead to the domination of the country by outsiders.

Belief in Spiritual Forces

Guiding the Athenians, Spartans, and the other ancient Greeks were their very strong beliefs in spiritual forces. They put their faith in a hierarchy of gods and believed all mortal actions on earth were directed

Citizens of ancient Greece take part in a procession honoring the goddess Athena. In politics, diplomacy, warfare, trade, and even daily life the ancient Greeks sought guidance from their many deities and took inspiration from the extraordinary accomplishments of their mythical heroes.

by the Greek deities. Moreover, the Greeks believed in elaborate myths that told stories of heroes who accomplished extraordinary deeds. The Greeks' decisions in politics, diplomacy, warfare, trade, and other aspects of life were often guided by how they believed their mythical heroes would have responded to such challenges or how they thought their gods wished them to act. If they needed guidance, Greek leaders often sought the advice of oracles—spiritualists who were thought to channel the commands of the gods. The oracles would advise the Greeks on the proper paths to take—more likely, they simply told their masters what they thought they wanted to hear. When the tiny city-state of Aigion captured an enemy's warship, the Aigian leaders consulted their oracle to determine the significance of the victory. The oracle responded that the Aigians were among the bravest warriors in Greece. "You, Aigians, are not [even] third or fourth [in bravery],"[4] the oracle concluded, suggesting that they were first or second among Greece's bravest warriors.

Despite their constant bickering and warfare, the Greeks excelled during the ancient era. For more than a thousand years, the Greeks conquered their enemies, controlled trade in the eastern Mediterranean Sea and generally improved the human condition in their society, including the introduction of the world's first democracy. Says Durant, "[In Greece], men had been lifted from barbarism to civilization by the passage of nomadic hunting to settled agriculture, by the replacement of stone tools with copper and bronze, by the conveniences of writing and the stimulation of trade."[5]

Chapter 1

What Conditions Led to the Rise of Ancient Greece?

Civilization first found its way to the Mediterranean peninsula known as Greece some 6,000 years ago as migrants traveled south from central Europe, west from Turkey and the Middle East, and north from Africa. The early history of Greece is hazy—historians have pieced together few facts about the first inhabitants of what in ancient times was known as Hellas, or "land of light." The name is derived from Helios, the ancient Greek god of the sun.

Indeed, historians have learned that much of the history of ancient Greece is wrapped in myth—stories about ancient Greek gods and heroes are intermingled with facts. The invasion of Greece by a tribe known as the Dorians provides a typical example.

The Dorians believed they were descended from Dorus, a son of Helen (daughter of the god Zeus) and a mortal woman, Leda. The Dorians emigrated from the Balkan region south of the Danube River into Greece around 1100 BC. They were a warlike people who had mastered the casting of iron into swords and shields, giving them an advantage in battle over their foes who fought with weapons cast in bronze—a much weaker metal. As they fought their way through Greece, the Dorians easily overran tiny settlements, turning their defeated foes into slaves. The Dorians built their first city in Corinth on the northern coast of Peloponnesus, a land mass in the southernmost portion of Greece. Peloponnesus is itself an 8,300-square-mile peninsula (29,417 sq. km) connected to the Greek mainland by the narrow Isthmus of Corinth. On Peloponnesus the Dorians would also establish a settlement known as Sparta, which later rose as one of the most powerful city-states in Greece.

Descendants of Heracles

While it would appear the Dorians possessed the weapons and fortitude to win battles entirely on their own, they were motivated by what to them was a much more powerful source of strength and courage. The Dorians believed they had a right to the lands they conquered because they were led by the descendants of Zeus's son Heracles, a hero renowned for his enormous strength and courage. (In popular culture Heracles is more widely known as Hercules, the Latin version of the name.) Moreover, the Dorians believed they were reclaiming land in Greece that had been denied to Heracles. The Dorian invasion is often known as the "Return of the Heracleidae." Says Will Durant,

> The victors were not content to record their triumph as a conquest of a civilized people by barbarians; they protested that what had really happened was that the descendants of Heracles, resisted in their just re-entry into Peloponnesus, had taken it by heroic force. We do not know how much of this is history, and how much of it is diplomatic mythology designed to transform a bloody conquest into a divine right. It is difficult to believe the Dorians were such excellent liars in the very youth of the world. Perhaps . . . both stories were true: the Dorians were conquerors from the north, led by the scions of Heracles.[6]

Earliest Settlements

There were residents of the Greek peninsula long before the Dorians and other invaders arrived. Archaeological evidence suggests people inhabited Greece as far back as 4000 BC during what was known as the

The Twelve Labors of Heracles

The ancient Greeks acknowledged Heracles as the strongest and bravest warrior in the land, but Zeus's wife, Hera, was angry at her husband's infidelity in conceiving the child with a mortal woman. To seek revenge, Hera vowed to torture Heracles throughout his life. In one episode she uses her power to make Heracles temporarily insane. In a rage, Heracles murders his wife and children.

To purge the guilt from his soul, Heracles consults Eurystheus, king of the city-state Mycenae and known throughout Greece for his intelligence. Eurystheus tells Heracles that he could absolve himself of guilt by performing twelve tasks—known as labors. They are extremely dangerous tasks; Eurystheus tells Heracles that he doubts a mortal could accomplish the deeds. Unknown to Heracles, Hera played a role in crafting the labors.

Among the tasks are battles with fearsome beasts, including the lion of Nemea; a nine-headed serpent known as the Hydra; a ferocious boar found on Mount Erymanthus; a deadly bull found on Crete; man-eating horses in Thrace, and the monster ox of Geryon.

The most difficult of the labors is the cleansing of the stables of Augeas, which held thousands of cattle and had not been cleaned for years. Heracles accomplishes the task by diverting the course of two rivers, flooding the stables, cleaning out years of accumulated filth. Heracles accomplished all 12 labors, but according to legend, he never purged his soul of guilt and always felt responsible for the deaths of his family.

Neolithic Age—or the final years of the Stone Age. Neolithic tribes established settlements along the coast of the Aegean Sea, the body of water that separates Greece from Turkey. Clearly, these tribes had the means to travel by water; the island of Crete, in the southernmost waters of the Aegean, grew quickly into an early center of Greek civilization around 1600 BC. "There is a land called Crete," wrote the ancient Greek poet Homer, "in the midst of the wine-dark sea, a fair, rich land, [surrounded] by water; and therein are many men past counting, and ninety cities."[7] Some of the earliest inhabitants of Crete are believed to have made the 400-mile (644km) Mediterranean Sea voyage from northern Africa—most likely from Egypt. In addition to the settlements in Peloponnesus, other early settlements were established in 1400 BC on the Cyclades, a group of islands in the Aegean Sea; and in Attica, a region on the southern mainland where the city-state Athens would rise around 1300 BC.

As the Dorians proved, establishment of these settlements was usually accomplished through the shedding of blood. The Greeks were a warlike people. They saw themselves as the human embodiments of the gods and heroes of their myths. The Trojan War serves as a prime example of the philosophy of the Greeks of this era. It also serves as another example of how the ancient Greek historians and storytellers were expected to weave myth into their retellings of actual events.

The Siege of Troy

The war was waged about 1250 BC between Greek invaders and defenders of Troy—also known as Troad or Troas—in the Anatolia region in western Turkey. The Greeks won the war, probably because they were better fighters and more merciless than the Trojan defenders, but the story of the Trojan War has been raised to the status of myth because of its retelling in the epic poems the *Iliad* and the *Odyssey* authored by Homer. (The years in which Homer lived and wrote the two poems have long been in dispute—historians believe the life of Homer dates anywhere from the mid-ninth century BC to the mid-seventh century BC).

According to Homer, the war commenced when Paris, son of the Trojan king Priam, kidnapped Helen, the wife of the Spartan king Menelaus (and mother of Dorus), spiriting her back to Troy. According to the legend, Paris appealed to Aphrodite, the Greek goddess of love, to lead him to the most beautiful woman in the world. Aphrodite responded by telling Paris the woman he sought was Helen. Paris sailed for Sparta. As the son of a king, Paris was accepted by Menelaus into his home, unaware of Paris's true intentions. Paris waited until Menelaus was called away to Crete and then, according to Homer, the Trojan

> Entered a friend's kind dwelling,
> Shamed the hand there that gave him food,
> Stealing away a woman.[8]

Menelaus raised an army of Greeks to sail to Troy and retrieve his wife. The army, which is said to have sailed to Troy in a fleet of 1,000 ships, was led by many of the most revered Greek heroes, including Achilles and Odysseus. Achilles is said to have been made nearly immortal when, as a baby, his mother, Thetis, dipped him into the mythical River Styx, which separates Earth from the underworld. Because Thetis held the child by the heel, he was only vulnerable in that part of his foot—a fact that Paris would exploit in the war when he killed Achilles by aiming an arrow at his heel. As for Odysseus, following the war he would go on to participate in many mythical adventures, including encounters with a giant one-eyed creature known as a Cyclops, the six-headed serpent Scylla, and a deadly whirlpool known as Charybdis.

Act of Mischief

Unable to breach the gates of the walled city of Troy, the Greeks found themselves in a stalemate against a powerful army. The Greeks encamped outside the gates of Troy and remained there for 10 years, finally finding a way to enter the city through a clever act of mischief. They convinced the Trojans of their intentions to abandon the siege and, before departing, erected a huge wooden horse and left it at the gates of the city as a curse

Escape from Troy

As the ancient Greeks built their civilization, another powerful nation had been founded nearby. That nation was Rome, located on the Italian Peninsula west of Greece. Rome would eventually grow into an empire that stretched from England to North Africa to the Middle East. According to the first-century BC Roman poet Virgil, Rome was founded by the Trojan Aeneas, who escaped the sack of Troy and led his followers to a new settlement in Italy along the banks of the Tiber River.

In Virgil's poem *The Aeneid*, the poet describes the discovery of the Trojan Horse and the suspicions of some Trojans that they should be wary of what lurks inside. In the poem the Trojan Laocoön says,

> O poor citizens, what madness so great
> Is this? You believe the enemy gone? You suppose
> Any gifts from the Greeks lack guile, . . .
> Some trick lies hidden within; do not trust in the horse.
> Whatever it is, I fear the Greeks even with gifts.

Laocoön thrusts a spear at the horse. When the spear strikes the wooden horse, the Trojans hear an echo. Still, they do not suspect the Trojan Horse contains enemy soldiers. Says Aeneas,

> If the Fates of the gods, if our minds, had not been unlucky,
> [Laocoön] would have [detected] the Greek hiding place
> with steel,
> And Troy would be standing.

Virgil, *The Aeneid, an Epic of Rome,* trans., Robert Lind Levi, Bloomington: Indiana University Press, 1962, p. 24.

on the Trojan people. A Greek emissary told the Trojans that the horse was a monument to the Greek goddess Athena and if they destroyed the horse, they would bring down the wrath of the goddess on their city. The Trojans fell into the trap and, instead of destroying the horse, chose to haul it inside their gates.

After the Greeks broke camp and retreated, the Trojans opened the gates and wheeled the huge wooden horse inside. "With song and rejoicing they brought death in. Treachery and destruction,"[9] wrote the Roman poet Virgil a thousand years later. Indeed, the Trojans did not know a small band of Greeks, led by Odysseus, was hiding inside the horse. When night fell, Odysseus led his men out of the horse and threw open the gates of Troy, enabling the Greek army to rush in. The Greeks ransacked the city and burned it to the ground. Priam was slain by the son of Achilles. Paris was killed by a Greek prince, Philoctetes, who is said to have used the bow and arrows of Heracles to slay Helen's kidnapper. Helen was returned to Menelaus, and together they sailed home for Greece.

Although that story may contain many mythical elements, a Trojan War did take place, and it was fought between the armies of Greece and Troy. In 1990 archaeologists unearthed evidence of the city of Troy, which was located near the confluence of the Dümrek and Karamenderes Rivers. They found remnants of a wooden wall that may have housed the gates of Troy as well as a trench that surrounded the city. The trench was likely used as a defense against chariot attacks.

The Greek attack on Troy, some experts say, might have had less to do with retrieving the beautiful wife of a king and more to do with concerns about Trojan control over trade through the nearby Dardanelles straits. During times of low tide, Greek merchant ships had to anchor at the entrance to the straits—where they were easy prey for Trojan tribute collectors. "We know from later texts that occupants of the region exacted tolls from incoming vessels," says Manfred Korfmann, an archaeologist at Tübingen University in Germany. "It is possible that Troy experienced several commercial skirmishes, if not one Trojan War."[10]

Unable to breach the gates of the walled city of Troy, the ancient Greeks came up with an elaborate ruse involving a small band of soldiers hidden inside a huge wooden horse. The unsuspecting Trojans brought the horse inside the gates. At nightfall, the hidden soldiers slipped out of the horse and opened the gates for the waiting Greek army.

Gods and Lesser Gods

Despite the evidence that trade disputes may have led to warfare between Greece and Troy, the story that has gained the most traction in history is the tale woven by Homer in the *Iliad* and the *Odyssey*, telling of the abduction of Helen and her rescue by the mythical heroes of Greece, among them Achilles and Odysseus. Says Michael Grant,

> These two poems . . . supplied the Greeks with their greatest civilizing influence, and formed the foundation of their literary, artistic, moral, social, educational and political attitudes. For a long time, no histories of early times seemed at all necessary, since the *Iliad* and the *Odyssey* fulfilled every requirement. They attracted

universal esteem and reverence, too, as sources of general and practical wisdom, as arguments for heroic yet human nobility and dignity, as incentives to vigorous (often bellicose) manly action.[11]

Indeed, the ancient Greeks allowed themselves to be guided by their gods and mythical heroes. The ancient Greeks were polytheists—believers in multiple gods. At the top of the hierarchy sat Zeus, the chief god, said to have attained his ruling status by drawing lots with his brothers Poseidon, god of the seas, and Hades, god of the underworld. Zeus was married to Hera, goddess of marriage. Their union produced a son, Ares, god of war. But Zeus was also a philanderer and fathered many other children, including Athena, goddess of agriculture; Apollo, the god of music, medicine, and light; Aphrodite, goddess of love and beauty; Hermes, the messenger god; and Artemis, goddess of the hunt. These gods and others are known as the Olympians—the major deities of ancient Greek belief. They ruled from atop Mount Olympus, the tallest mountain in Greece (although Hades oversaw his realm of the dead in the underworld.)

The Greeks also believed in numerous of the so-called lesser gods. These gods had specific roles that affected the lives of mortals. Iris was a granddaughter of Poseidon; she was charged with conveying Zeus's orders to the other gods and is said to have spoken to mortals as well. Several gods, daughters of Zeus known as the Graces—among them Euphrosyne, Aglaia, and Thalia—brought happiness and inspiration to the lives of mortals and also provided the earth with flowers and fruit. The three goddesses known as the Horae were the guardians of the gates of Olympus. The lesser goddesses known as the Muses guided the creation of music and other intellectual achievements by mortals. The Greeks believed there were a total of nine Muses; among them were Calliope, the Muse of epic poetry; Erato, Muse of love poetry; Melpomene, Muse of tragedy, and Terpsichore, Muse of dance.

Other lesser gods carried out specific tasks on land, in the sky, and under the sea. The goddess Selene stood guard over the moon while other lesser gods, the Keres, followed warriors to their deaths in battle or through other violent means. The goddess Herse created the morning dew. The god Poros brought wealth to mortals while the goddess Penia had the power to turn rich men into paupers. The lesser god Eros brought love to mortals: The popular image of Eros is that of a young winged child, armed with bow and arrows. That image has survived the centuries, as anyone who has opened a Valentine's Day card can attest. (The Romans called their version of this god Cupid, a name more familiar in popular culture.)

The goddesses known as the Sirens led sailors to their deaths. They had human heads and the bodies of birds. When sailors heard them singing, the doomed men were sure to crash their ships and drown. In the *Odyssey* Homer writes that as Odysseus returns to Greece following the Trojan War, his ship nears the island where the Sirens are said to dwell. Odysseus commands his men to stuff wax into their ears so they would not hear the song of the Sirens.

The Birth of Heracles

Some of these stories may carry an element of fright, but the Greeks did not fear their gods; they looked to them for guidance. "The world of Greek mythology was not a place of terror for the human spirit," says historian Edith Hamilton. "It is true that the gods were disconcertingly incalculable. One could never tell where Zeus's thunderbolt would strike. Nevertheless, the whole divine company, with a very few and for the most part not important exceptions, were entrancingly beautiful with a human beauty, and nothing humanly beautiful is really terrifying. The early Greek mythologists transformed a world full of fear into a world full of beauty."[12]

Some of the Greek myths told the stories of how mortals responded to challenges posed to them by the gods. Heracles was the son of Zeus, but his mother, Alcmena, was mortal. He possessed great strength and courage but was mortal in all other respects. Hera, angry at Zeus for his infidelity, resolved to kill Heracles. When he was a baby, asleep in his crib, Hera sent two poisonous snakes into the child's room. As the snakes slithered into his crib, Heracles suddenly awoke, grasped the two snakes by their throats and choked the life out of them. After learning of the baby's strength and courage, the oracle Teiresias told Alcmena, "I swear that many a Greek woman as she [cleans] the wool at eveningtide shall sing of this your son and you who bore him. He shall be the hero of all mankind."[13]

Quest for the Golden Fleece

Although Teiresias left little doubt about who would become Greece's most courageous hero, other heroes of myth also performed deeds that would long be admired by the ancient Greeks. Jason was a prince of the city-state Iolcus. His father, the rightful king of Iolcus, was ousted by his brother Pelias and kept imprisoned. To protect Jason from Pelias, his mother sent him into the wilderness to be raised by the centaur Chiron. (A centaur has the body of a horse but the torso, arms, and head of a human.) When he reached adulthood, Jason returned to Iolcus to claim the throne.

Pelias had no intention of turning his reign over to Jason so he issued a challenge: Jason could claim the throne of Iolcus if he retrieved a fleece—the hide and wool of a ram—made of gold. Jason agreed to the challenge. He had a ship built by the master shipbuilder Argus and recruited a crew of the bravest men in Greece. The crew boarded the ship, known as the *Argo*, and set sail. To guide the ship, Jason appealed to Hera, who agreed to protect the "Argonauts" and guide them to their destination.

Along the way Jason and the Argonauts fought off the Harpies, flying lizard-like creatures, and navigated through the dangerous clashing rocks known as the Symplegades. Finally, the voyage led the Argonauts to Colchis, a kingdom in what is now the nation of Georgia, located just north of Turkey.

King Aietes of Colchis refused to give up the fleece—an oracle had advised Aietes that if he lost the fleece, he would lose his throne. And so Aietes set what he was sure was an impossible condition for the relinquishment of the fleece: Jason would first have to dig furrows into a field by harnessing two killer bulls to a plow. After accomplishing this chore Jason and his men must slay a serpent, then plant the serpent's teeth in the furrows. From these planted teeth an army of warriors would grow. To win the fleece the Argonauts would have to defeat the children of the serpent's teeth.

Jason accepted the challenge. He knew Hera would assist him. In fact, Hera had already appealed to Aphrodite, who made Aietes's daughter—the sorceress Medea—fall in love with Jason. Using a secret potion concocted by Medea that made him invulnerable to the attacks by the bulls, Jason was able to harness the fearsome animals and dig the furrows.

When Jason planted the teeth, a band of armed warriors grew out of the furrows. But the Argonauts would not have to fight these soldiers: Using his guile, Jason convinced these newly hatched warriors to be suspicious of each other. They fought among themselves, finally killing one another.

Medea led Jason to the tree whose limbs held the golden fleece. The tree was guarded by a dragon. Medea uttered a magical charm that put the dragon to sleep. Jason snatched the fleece from the tree and, together with Medea, sailed home for Iolcus where Jason claimed the throne. Alas, Jason and Medea would not live happily ever after: According to the legend, Jason was also something of a philanderer.

Beasts of Greek Mythology

The story of the golden fleece tells of ferocious beasts that must be tamed by Jason. Such horrible characters were not confined to Jason's story. The mythology concocted by the ancient Greeks also included the story of Odysseus and the Cyclops Polyphemus, a one-eyed giant. While returning from the Trojan War, Odysseus and his men land in an unknown territory and search for food. They encounter the Cyclops, who imprisons them in his cave with the intention of eating them. Odysseus rescues his men by offering the Cyclops a bowl of wine. Polyphemus had never tasted wine; he finds it delicious and asks for more. Soon, Polyphemus falls asleep in a drunken stupor. As the Cyclops snoozes, Odysseus and his men carve a huge stake and drive it into the giant's eye, blinding him. The next day, Polyphemus pushes the boulder aside that blocks his cave entrance, allowing his sheep to graze in a nearby field. Odysseus and his men hide under the bellies of the sheep,

Perseus is the clear victor in the ancient Greek tale of his encounter with the fearsome Gorgons. In this illustration from the late nineteenth century, Perseus holds the severed head of Medusa and threatens two other Gorgons with the same fate.

enabling them to be undetected as the blinded Cyclops gropes among the animals, searching for the Greeks.

Just as fearsome as the Cyclops are the Gorgons, who are powerful winged creatures. Among the Gorgons is Medusa, whose scalp grows snakes rather than hair. Those who gaze directly on Medusa are turned to stone. To slay the Gorgon, the hero Perseus uses a shield—supplied by the goddess Athena, a daughter of Zeus—that shines so sharply it reflects the image of Medusa. Perseus was able to cut off the Gorgon's head by peering at her reflection in his shield.

Another beast of Greek mythology is the Minotaur of Crete. According to the story, to end the constant state of warfare between Crete and Athens, the Athenian ruler offers to send 14 children to Crete to be sacrificed to the Minotaur. The creature has the body of a man and head of a bull, and it dwells in an underground maze, or labyrinth. King Minos of Crete agrees to the terms, ending the long war.

When the time arrives for the children to be sacrificed, the Athenian prince Theseus offers to take the place of one of the doomed victims. He intends to kill the Minotaur. When the children arrive on Crete, the princess Ariadne meets Theseus and immediately falls in love with him. As Theseus and the children enter the maze, Ariadne gives Theseus a ball of string and a sword. Theseus uses the string to mark his route through the maze so that he can find his way out by following the string back to the entrance. When he finally faces the Minotaur, Theseus uses the sword given to him by Ariadne to slay the beast.

Wisdom of the Gods

Throughout their 1,100-year rule, the ancient Greeks believed these stories. To the Greeks, these stories illustrated how the gods guided mortals as they faced difficult decisions. And in ancient Greece, the solutions found in the wisdom of the gods often involved the use of the sword, which is why the courage, intelligence, and strength of heroes like Heracles, Jason, Theseus, and Perseus were held in such high regard by the Greeks. Belief in these stories would also go a long way toward explaining why the mortal Greeks were so willing to use their swords and armies to settle their differences.

Chapter 2

Rise of the City-States

To the ancient Greeks, the Battle of Thermopylae stands out as their finest moment of glory. Although the battle ended in a loss for the Greeks, the 300 Spartans and their allies who held out against an overwhelming force of Persian invaders are regarded as folk heroes. Moreover, the campaign to defend Greece against the Persian invaders represents one of the few times in the history of ancient Greece that its two most powerful city-states, or poleis, managed to put their differences aside and ally themselves against a common enemy.

The battle was waged in 480 BC. To avenge a humiliating defeat suffered a decade before, the Persian king, Xerxes, amassed an invasion force said to number in the tens of thousands. The invaders sailed across the Mediterranean, arriving on Greece's eastern shores. As the Persians fought their way across the country, several thousand approached the narrow mountain pass of Thermopylae on the Isthmus of Corinth. They were met by a force of just 300 Spartans as well as 700 soldiers from the city-state Thespiae. Although greatly outnumbered, Greece's most fearsome warriors held off the overwhelming force of Persians for three days. According to the legend, the Persians lost some 20,000 soldiers attempting to fight their way through the tiny mountain pass.

The battle was lost when the Spartans were betrayed by Ephialtes, a Greek who sought reward from the Persians for showing them a secret path around Thermopylae. Now the Persians could attack the Spartans and their Thespian allies from the front and rear. The defenders were soon slaughtered—all 300 Spartans died in the battle, including their king, Leonidas, whose body was mutilated by the Persian invaders. All the Thespian soldiers lost their lives as well.

The Persians may have prevailed at Thermopylae, but they ultimately lost what is known as the Second Greco-Persian War. A superior fleet of Athenian ships, known as triremes, destroyed the Persian navy near the island of Cyprus. As the Persian sailors jumped off their burning ships and swam to shore, they were met by Spartan swordsmen who cut them down as vengeance for the slaughter at Thermopylae.

After the war, the Battle of Thermopylae was recorded by the fifth century BC historian Herodotus who wrote that the 300 Spartans are buried beneath the battlefield and that those who come across their graves are to heed this message:

> Stranger, report this word, we pray, to the Spartans, that lying
> Here in this spot, we remain, faithfully still keeping their laws.[14]

No Single Ruler

In fact, the law of the Spartans was clear: Spartan men were raised as warriors. They lived in barracks, apart from their wives and children. They constantly trained in the art of warfare and were expected to maintain courage in battle and follow their leaders with unquestioning loyalty. Because of their ferocity and fearlessness, they were able to build Sparta into one of the premier city-states in ancient Greece.

In the ancient era, Greece was not unified under a single ruler. In fact, Greece was not even the name of the country—it was Hellas, and the Greeks referred to themselves as Hellenes. The name for Greece stems from Latin, the language of the ancient Romans, who used the term *Graici* to describe the people of Hellas. It is likely the Romans based their name for the Greeks on a small Hellenic tribe known as the Graii who migrated to the Italian Peninsula. "The Romans gave to all Hellenes whom they encountered the name *Graici*," says Will Durant, "and from that circumstance all the world came to know Hellas by a term which its own inhabitants never applied to themselves."[15]

The Spartan king, Leonidas, bids farewell to his allies before the Battle of Thermopylae. Leonidas and his troops held off thousands of Persian soldiers for three days, but he and his men were slaughtered after a traitor showed the Persians a route around a narrow mountain pass.

Many Different Customs

Certainly, emperors and kings could be found in other corners of the ancient world, such as Persia and Egypt or, later, Rome. Instead, the tribes that had migrated to Greece over the centuries established self-governing settlements. Some grew into mighty city-states in control of vast swaths of territory, such as Sparta and Athens.

The cultures of the city-states developed on their own. Apart from a common language and beliefs in gods and myths, the Greek city-states shared little else. They wrote their own laws and observed their own customs. For example, the women of Sparta enjoyed many more freedoms than the women of Athens. In Athens, women were expected to stay in their homes all day—a woman who was seen on the street was regarded as a prostitute. Athenian women were permitted to own property, such as clothes, jewels, and slaves, but were not permitted to buy anything or inherit property from their families. The husband or father of an Athenian woman made all the decisions that affected her life.

Unlike Athenian women, Spartan women were permitted to leave their homes and encouraged to pursue athletic skills. Also unlike Athenian women, Spartan women were permitted to inherit property from their families. "To the ancient Greeks, Hellas meant every place occupied by Greeks, in which the Greek tongue was spoken and a certain sense of common origin and religion maintained," says historian Thomas George Tucker. "Indeed, beyond the possession of a common tongue—although this had its dialects, often as distinct from one another as Scotch [is] from standard English [and] a general similarity of dress and religion . . . it would be hard to say anything which would be equally applicable to all those whom we call the ancient Greeks."[16]

A Most Attractive City

The Spartans may have built a powerful city-state and offered their women more rights than women enjoyed in Athens, but Athens was powerful as well and rivaled Sparta as the premier polis of Greece. Athens is located in the south of Greece near the tip of a narrow peninsula known as Attica. The Athenians carved out a much different culture than the Spartans. Although they certainly never backed down from a fight, the Athenians had many nonmilitary interests. The Athenians labored as farmers, craftspeople, and tradespeople. There was also a class of wealthy aristocrats who ruled Athens.

Over the centuries Athens had grown into a center of trade and commerce—its central marketplace, the agora, was the busiest in Greece. Says Tucker, "Athens was in no sense the capital of ancient Greece. It happens to be the most attractive city, and the city of which we know most; it was the city in which art, intellect, and social culture flourished best, and therefore it has left us the completest records of itself. It was also the most populous city, and one of the most powerful."[17]

Rise of a Despot

By the middle of the sixth century BC, the Athenian ruler—known as the archon—was Peisistratus, an aristocrat who gained the favor of the Athenian people by lowering their taxes and giving them free land for farms. Under Peisistratus the city-state flourished and grew. When Peisistratus died in 527 BC, his son Hippias seized control of Athens and established himself as a dictator and despot. When Hippias's brother Hipparchus was murdered, the archon had the conspirators arrested and executed. He also tortured and murdered Leaena, the wife of a conspirator. According to Greek legend, while undergoing the harshest of tortures Leaena is said to have bitten off her own tongue and spat it in the face of her torturers—a defiant gesture that ensured she would not answer their questions.

Hippias grew suspicious of the Athenian aristocrats, believing they were conspiring against him. He had many members of the wealthy class banished from Athens. As for the working people and farmers of Athens, the freedoms and prosperity they had enjoyed under Peisistratus disappeared under their new ruler. Says Durant, "As the dictatorship grew harsher, the cry for freedom grew louder."[18]

As Hippias descended into madness, the aristocrat Cleisthenes planned to overthrow the ruler and seize power. He made his move in 510 BC, enlisting other aristocrats in a conspiracy and banishing Hippias, who fled to Persia.

The rule of Cleisthenes did not last long. Other wealthy Athenians conspired against him and, led by the aristocrat Isagoras, toppled Cleisthenes and banished him from Athens along with hundreds of others whom Isagoras suspected of tyranny. Isagoras was able to topple Cleisthenes with the help of the Spartans, who sent an army to prop up the new Athenian ruler. The Spartans had their own intentions—they intended to turn Athens into a city under their control.

For two years the citizens of Athens seethed under Spartan domination. Finally, in 508 BC the Athenians rose up in rebellion. Rioters took to the streets of Athens. Meanwhile, the Athenian rebels employed some trickery—they bribed the Spartans' oracle to tell the Spartan commanders to withdraw their support for Isagoras. During

How Sparta and Athens Were Named

As with most tales involving the ancient Greeks, the stories behind the naming of Sparta and Athens are mixtures of fact and myth. Historians attribute the founding of Sparta to the Dorians, who entered Greece in about 1100 BC. According to Greek legend, the polis was founded by Lacedaemon, a son of Zeus and a lesser goddess, Taygete. Lacedaemon married Sparta, and honored his wife by giving her name to the city. Sparta was the daughter of Eurotas, a lesser god of the river in Greece that bears his name.

The original Athenians occupied the territory as far back as 1400 BC. According to Greek mythology, as the settlement grew, its king, Cecrops, sought a deity to protect the village. Two of the Olympian gods, Poseidon and Athena, offered their protection. Cecrops told the two gods that he would select a divine protector based on their gifts to the village.

Poseidon responded by hurling his trident into the earth, opening an enormous well to supply drinking water to the villagers. But when the people tasted the water, they found it salty. Athena threw her spear into the ground. When the goddess withdrew the spear, an olive tree grew from the hole. To Cecrops and his people, the olive tree represented peace as well as a source for food, so they chose Athena as their protector and named their village Athens.

the uprising, Isagoras and his Spartan soldiers took refuge atop the Acropolis, a large, rocky hill in Athens. Isagoras and the Spartans managed to hold out for two days but on the third day surrendered to the angry Athenian mob, who exiled them from the city.

The Reforms of Solon

The Athenians asked Cleisthenes to return and take over the rule of their city. Cleisthenes agreed, but soon after arriving in Athens he realized the danger of entrusting one ruler with absolute authority. He decided to give the Athenians a say in their own welfare.

For the Athenians, the road toward democracy had been paved some 80 years before in 594 BC during the reign of the archon Solon. When Solon rose to power in Athens, the city-state was on the verge of civil war. A small minority of wealthy aristocrats owned most of the farmland that surrounded the city. The land that remained under the control of ordinary farmers was shrinking in value: As these farmers died, their land was subdivided among their surviving sons. Over the years the individual plots of land became smaller and smaller until many of these farms could no longer grow crops in a volume that made them profitable.

Many farmers were forced to buy grain from the aristocrats, putting the farmers in debt. In ancient Athens, failure to pay off a debt was regarded as a severe crime. To pay off his debt, the farmer often had to agree to be sold into slavery. A farmer in debt could also lose his land to his creditors and, even after paying off his debts, the farmer was still obligated to turn over a sixth of his crop to the aristocrat who made the original loan. In Athens the system was known as "debt-bondage."

Solon saw the damage the system was inflicting on the farming community of Athens. He could also see the unrest and unhappiness of the farmers who were in debt. After assuming the position of archon, Solon canceled all debts and ordered the aristocrats to return the farms to their original owners. Farmers sold into slavery were immediately granted their freedom. Solon also put limits on the amount of interest the wealthy aristocrats could charge on the loans they made to farmers as well as other citizens of Athens.

Rights of the Individual

The aristocrats of Athens were angered by these orders, but Solon, a talented statesman, convinced his critics that the old system of debt-bondage would eventually lead Athens into chaos. Solon told the aristocrats that unless the debt-bondage system was repealed, the farmers and other poor people would one day rise up against their creditors—a situation that could end in bloodshed for the aristocrats.

By defending the lowly citizens of Athens, Solon had established an important precedent: He had given rights to a class of people who had never before been permitted to exercise authority over the wealthier citizens of Athens. And so, by the time Cleisthenes accepted the office of archon, the citizens of Athens enjoyed a measure of individual rights unknown anywhere else in the world.

Solon died in 558 BC at the age of 80, after having served as archon for 36 years. "It was his greatest satisfaction that, despite all pressure, he had refused to accept the dictatorship of Athens," says Michael Grant. "He wanted the people to be contented, but did not want to order them, or to tell them how to achieve this condition [of contentment]; they must find out for themselves."[19]

The First Democracy

Cleisthenes intended to take Solon's reforms a step further. He ordered a meeting place carved out of the rock of an Athenian hillside. He decided that every issue that would be faced by the Athenian people would be discussed in public and all Athenians had a right to participate in the debate. These issues could be as minor as setting the price for figs or as important as building roads, assessing taxes, or declaring war.

Moreover, he instituted a system in which Athenians would vote and the majority ruled. During the assemblies, Athenians would cast their votes in the form of white pebbles if they agreed with the motion, black pebbles if they disagreed. As the archon, Cleisthenes served as the chief executive carrying out the wishes of the assembly, much as the US president carries out the laws established by Congress.

Cleisthenes had established history's first democracy—a word derived from the Greek words *demos*, which means "people," and *kratos*, which means "power." Today's democracies typically do not resemble the Athenian model. In most modern democratic countries, voters elect representatives to assemblies—such as the US Congress or British Parliament. These are known as representative democracies—the representatives elected by the people vote on issues and make laws. Nevertheless, the Athenian Assembly is democracy in its purest form—the lowliest laborer in Athens held as much power in the assembly as the wealthiest aristocrat: Each was permitted a single vote. Says Will Durant, "The Athenians themselves were exhilarated by this adventure into sovereignty. They realized that they had undertaken a difficult enterprise, but they advanced to it with courage and pride. . . . From that moment they knew the zest for freedom and thought; and from that moment they began to lead all Greece in literature and art, even in statesmanship and war."[20]

Warfare Common in Greece

Other city-states of Greece soon adopted Athenian-style democracy as well. Among these city-states were Ambraca, Megara, Chios, Cyrene, Heraclea Pontica, Mantinea, and Naxos. Others, including Sparta, clung to the autocratic rule of their kings. Greece is believed to have contained some 1,500 to 2,000 city-states during the ancient era; they were all ruled by their individual assemblies, kings, or archons.

Whether they were governed by assemblies or monarchs, Greek city-states were suspicious of one another and often outwardly hostile. Warfare among the city-states was common. The tiny island of Ceos in the Aegean Sea was home to four city-states that constantly waged war among themselves. Sparta shared the Peloponnesian Peninsula with Argos, but the two poleis were bitter enemies and regular combatants. The city-states of Plataea and Sybaris fought so much that they finally destroyed each other. The Athenians sought to annex all the city-states on the Attica Peninsula, among them Mende, Torone, and Scione. To accomplish this goal, Athens sent armies to sack their neighboring poleis. In many such wars, the losers would be slaughtered by the vanquishing armies or taken home as slaves.

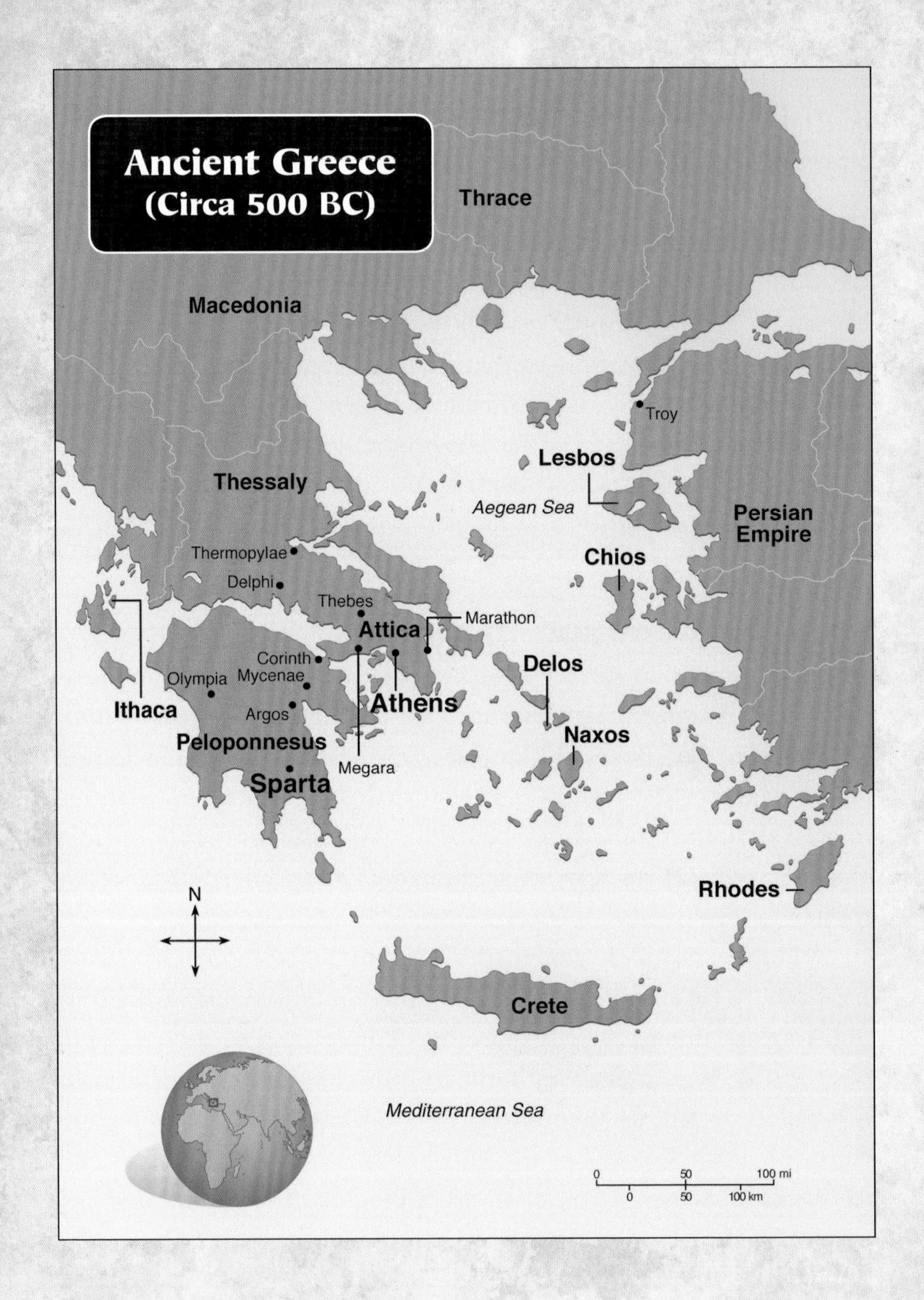

The Battle of Marathon

The city-states that adopted democracy flourished under their chosen form of government, particularly Athens. The Persians looked at the wealth accumulated by the Athenians and intended to seize it for themselves. By the beginning of the fifth century BC, Darius, the ruler of Persia (now known as Iran) had expanded his empire westward to include parts of Europe, southward to North Africa, and eastward to India. He started the first Greco-Persian war by attacking Greek settlements along the coast of Turkey. In 490 BC a fleet of Persian warships sailed for Greece. Learning that the Persians intended to land their navy at a Greek coastal town known as Marathon, the Athenians appealed to the Spartans for help. A young Athenian officer, Pheidippides, was given the task of summoning the Spartans. He ran some 140 miles from Marathon to Sparta, covering the distance in two days. The Spartans agreed to aid the Athenians but were—perhaps purposely—tardy in their response.

Although the Spartans arrived at Marathon too late to help, the Athenians were able to defeat the Persians on their own. An army of 20,000 Athenians—half the population of the city—was mustered for the Battle of Marathon. They faced an invading army of 100,000 Persians. The Athenians fought relentlessly, killing 6,000 Persians on the first day. The Persians soon left Greece in defeat. Against tremendous odds, the Athenians had prevailed at Marathon. Pheidippides, who had returned to Marathon, ran back to Athens—a distance of 26 miles—to announce the victory. According to legend, the exhausted runner announced the Athenian victory with his dying breath.

Military historians have argued for centuries over the reasons for the Greek victory against a superior force of Persians. Most attribute the Greek victory to the tactics employed by their commanders—they sent wedges of well-trained warriors known as hoplites into undisciplined hordes of Persian soldiers. The Greek soldiers were heavily armed and armored and were trained to fight in formation—usually in tightly-formed V-shaped units known as phalanxes. They kept their shields high and pushed into the enemy ranks with the aim of splitting their opponents into small groups, making them vulnerable. Thus, the long-held military strategy to divide and conquer finds its roots in ancient Greece. Says California State University historian Victor Davis Hanson, "Hoplite fighting through shock collision marks the true beginning of western warfare."[21]

The Greek style of fighting was pioneered by the Spartans, but eventually all Greek city-states trained their soldiers as hoplites. The namc has its root in the Greek word *hopla*, which means heavy battle gear.

The Triremes of Athens

Although the Spartans fell defending the mountain pass at Thermopylae, the tide of the war soon turned against the Persians—thanks largely to the might of the Athenian navy. Following the first war against Persia in 490 BC, the Athenian general Themistocles warned that the threat of a Persian invasion remained. Rather than build up the Athenian army to meet the Persians on land, Themistocles proposed building a powerful navy that could fight the Persian vessels at sea. The assembly agreed, and Themistocles was given the task of developing the Athenian navy.

Under Themistocles, the Athenians built a fleet of some 400 ships known as triremes. Each ship required 170 rowers manning three banks of oars—hence the name. (The word is derived from the Greek term *trieres*, which means "three-fitted.") The ships were 120 feet (36.6m) long and 20 feet (6m) wide. The vessels were fast and very maneuverable. The front of the ship was made of solid wood and used as a battering ram. "There has probably never been as bizarre yet successful a galley as the Greek trireme," says California State University historian Victor Davis Hanson. "The crew could row at 50 strokes a minute to achieve short bursts of fighting speeds . . . as it delivered devastating force with its ram."

Victor Davis Hanson, *A War Like No Other: How the Athenians and Spartans Fought the Peloponnesian War*. New York: Random House, 2005, pp. 236–37.

Culture of War

Although the Greek soldiers may have employed superior tactics and weaponry over the Persians at Marathon, some historians suggest the Athenians had more to fight for—they were defending their newfound freedoms and their democracy. The Persians, on the other hand, were fighting under the orders of their king. "Every battle has some effect on history," says military historian William Weir. "Most people would put freedom and democracy high on any list of desirable things. Consequently, Marathon, which preserved the world's first democracy, holds the number-one spot."[22]

As both Sparta and Athens rose in power, they grew even more envious and distrusting of each other. The other city-states of Greece suffered similar degrees of jealousy and suspicion. During the era of ancient Greece, the entire country would never be united under a single Greek assembly or monarch. This refusal to unite would often lead the city-states into war. Indeed, warfare was so common in ancient Greece that every man—aristocrat, farmer, craftsman, and laborer—was expected to answer his city-state's call to arms. Perhaps Heraclitus, a fifth-century BC Greek philosopher, did the best job of defining his country's main preoccupation. He called war, "The father of all, the king of all."[23]

Chapter 3

An Era of Achievement

Every four years, ancient Greece's greatest athletes gathered outside the city of Olympia in Peloponnesus for a series of competitions, including footraces, wrestling matches, long jumps, javelin throws, discus throws, chariot races, and other events. It is believed the first of the Olympic Games were held in 776 BC. As with most chapters in ancient Greek history, the origin of the Olympics is intermingled with myth: Heracles is said to have organized the first competitions.

However the games started, they were extremely popular because not only would athletes head for the Olympics but thousands of spectators looked forward to the events as well. Many people traveled for weeks to attend the games; as many as 50,000 camped outside the city for the five days of the competitions. During the Olympics, the city-states of Greece—often at war and almost always suspicious of one another—put aside their differences so that their athletes could compete against one another in a spirit of unity.

To enable the large crowds to attend, the games were staged in August or September, a time period between the end of the grain harvest and the beginning of the harvest for grapes and olives. No treasures were awarded to the competitors—the only awards granted to the winners were wreaths of laurel leaves, which were placed on their heads following their events. (Of course, when they returned home they found themselves revered as local heroes and honored by their city-states for the rest of their lives.)

Moreover, the spirit of the Olympics would serve as an inspiration to Cleisthenes as he established the world's first democracy in Athens:

At the Olympics athletes from all walks of life were permitted to compete against one another. Farmers, laborers, craftsmen, and aristocrats could all enter the same competitions: Each athlete was judged not on his personal wealth, education, or birthright but by his ability to run, wrestle, or throw the discus. At the Olympics everyone was treated as an equal, as they would be treated in the Athenian Assembly.

The Olympics represented not only an opportunity for individuals to achieve great deeds but for ancient Greek society itself to set an important precedent that has been followed into modern times. All modern sports—not only the modern version of the Olympics but all other sports as well, including football, baseball, soccer, basketball, and hockey—are waged on highly competitive levels, typically in front of crowds that number in the tens of thousands. In most cases teams represent cities, and the successes of those teams have a lot to do with the measure of civic pride found in their home cities.

The Grecian Urn

The staging of the Olympics illustrates that more than just warfare and mythology dominated the lives of the ancient Greeks. Indeed, as the Greeks were fighting off the Persians or fighting each other, many citizens of ancient Greece were providing important discoveries in science, mathematics, the arts, and literature.

Ancient Greece was an agrarian society—most people were farmers. The land of Greece, particularly in the region surrounding Athens, was suitable for the growing of olives. Athens became a major trading center, shipping its olives to other countries such as Egypt, Phoenicia, Persia, and Assyria. The olives were a source of food but they could also be milled into oil, which could be used for cooking, lighting, and as a lubricant. To store the olive oil, large urns were needed, and so the craft of the potter became an important trade in ancient Greece. Soon, the Grecian urn became more than just a receptacle for olive oil. The ancient Greek potters decorated the urns with images of gods, stories of important battles, and deeds of mythical heroes.

Athletes and spectators gathered outside Olympia every four years for a series of sports competitions that became known as the Olympic Games. The games included footraces (pictured), wrestling matches, javelin and discus throws, and other events.

The art of Greek pottery first emerged in the early part of the sixth century BC. Craftsmen in Corinth are believed to have been the first to fashion so-called black-figure pottery. The urns were fashioned from red clay. Using black paint, the potters applied the artistic scenes. Soon, Athenian artisans adopted these methods and produced Grecian urns valued for their beauty. In about 530 BC the Athenian potters developed the "red-figure" method. This method required the artisan to paint the background black, leaving the figures and scenes depicted on the surface in the natural red color.

Some ceramists eschewed scenes of myth and battle for scenes of everyday life showing children at play, men attending banquets, or athletes in competition. Other types of pottery—those designed to hold water or wine—also contained artistic images. "[A] mighty artistic sixth-century accomplishment, in which, even if Corinth had been the pioneer, Athens later took an unchallenged lead, was the uniquely rich, rapid and varied evolution of painting on pottery," says Michael Grant. "Black-figure and early red-figure master-painters achieved heights of power and moving beauty of which the medium has never again found itself capable."[24]

The *Discus Thrower*

Pottery was only one form of art mastered by the ancient Greeks. Sculpture and painting also developed into major art forms under Greek artists. As with the potters, the ancient Greek sculptors sought to honor gods and heroes in their work. A typical example is the *Discobolos*, or the *Discus Thrower*, cast in bronze in 470 BC by the Athenian sculptor Myron. As described by Will Durant, "The wonder of the male frame is here complete: the body carefully studied in all those movements of muscle, tendon, and bone that are involved in the action; the legs and arms and trunk bent to give the fullest force to the throw; the face not distorted with effort, but calm in the confidence of ability; the head not heavy or brutal, but that of a man of blood and refinement."[25]

The golden age of ancient Greek painting occurred during the fourth and fifth centuries BC. During this era, Greek painters responded to the demands of the aristocrats to decorate their homes with murals, known as frescoes, or portraits painted on cloths or boards. The Greek artists may have been the first to use oil paints—they mixed their colors with melted wax, which in the ancient era contained olive oil.

As with urns, Greek paintings often depicted battles and other historical events or scenes from mythical tales. In 472 BC one noted Greek artist, Polygnotus, was commissioned to adorn the walls of several buildings in Athens with frescoes. Along the wall of the Athens stoa—a public walkway—Polygnotus painted a scene from the Trojan War. He chose not to paint a scene from a battle or a depiction of the Trojans hauling the wooden horse into their city, but a scene illustrating the aftermath of the sack of Troy: Greek soldiers standing amid the bodies of dead Trojans. Later, Polygnotus was commissioned by the city-state Delphi to paint a number of murals; in one fresco he depicted the hero Odysseus visiting the underworld. On the wall of the Delphi *lesche*—a public lounge common in the ancient Greek world—he painted another scene from the Trojan War, depicting a Greek ship departing Troy. In the center of the ship sat Helen, surrounded by other women who gaze upon her beauty.

Construction of the Parthenon

In addition to sculpture and art, the ancient Greeks were also pioneers in architecture. Each city-state erected a temple dedicated to a god. Of course, since most of the city-states were jealous of one another, when it came to erecting their temples each polis attempted to outdo its neighbors. "All the Greek world was building temples in this period," says Will Durant. "Cities almost bankrupted themselves in rivalry to have the fairest statuary and the largest shrines."[26]

A common form of design during the ancient Greek era was so-called Doric architecture. Introduced by the Dorians, Doric buildings are recognized by their bold and numerous columns. The Doric column does not feature a base. At the top, the column is headed by a crown known as a capital. Running along the top of the columns are long walls of stone, usually decorated with friezes—sculptures etched into a flat surface. Atop the friezes sit the roofs, which are slanted.

The Greek Chorus

The tragedies and comedies of the ancient Greek theater always featured what is known as the "Greek Chorus." The chorus was composed of nonprofessional actors; their job was to provide a running commentary during the play. The chorus leader, known as the coryphaeus, engaged in dialogue with the actors. Chorus members also sang and danced when required by the script.

The chorus did not share the stage with the actors. Rather, the chorus members took their places below the stage in an area the Greeks called the "orchestra." Chorus members started the play by reciting a chant or singing a song as they marched into the theater to take their places in the orchestra. They wore costumes and usually masks. Women were not permitted to be chorus members.

The size of the chorus was up to the playwright. Sophocles preferred a chorus of 15, while Aeschylus preferred 12 members of the chorus. Says historian Will Durant, "The chorus is in many ways the most dramatic as well as the most costly aspect of the spectacle. . . . They dance as well as sing, and move in dignified procession across the long and narrow stage, interpreting through the poetry of motion the words and moods of the play."

Will Durant, *The Story of Civilization,* vol. 2: *The Life of Greece*. New York: Simon & Schuster, 1966, p. 379.

The most impressive of the ancient Greek temples was the Parthenon, erected under the orders of the Athenian archon Pericles. Pericles envisioned a great marble temple to honor the goddess Athena, to whom the city of Athens was dedicated. Pericles chose the Acropolis as the site for the temple. A smaller temple had been located atop the hill, but it had been burned to the ground by a Persian invasion years before. Work on the temple commenced in 447 BC and would take more than 20 years to complete.

The Parthenon was composed of 20,000 tons (18,144 metric tons) of white marble, keeping Athenian quarries busy for years as workers dug the stone needed for the massive building. The finest artists, sculptors, and craftsmen were employed to decorate the building. Inside, visitors could find a 500-foot-long frieze (152.4m) displaying events in Greek history and mythology. Greeting visitors at the entrance to the building was a 40-foot statue (12m) of Athena, decorated in gold, ivory, and jewels. Says art historian Jenifer Neils, "[The Partheon] conjures the glory of the classical past, Western civilization, and even democracy. Its image graces hundreds of publications from travel magazines to art history textbooks. It looks clean, white, and glistening in the Mediterranean sun. This is the Parthenon—the icon of Everyman."[27]

A lighted view of the Parthenon at night offers a reminder of the glories of ancient Greece. The Greeks placed great value on art and literature, architecture and philosophy, and math and science.

Another facet of Greek art could be found on the stage. This was the era of the Greek tragedy and the work of the playwrights Aristophanes, Euripides, Aeschylus, and Sophocles, all of whom lived in the fourth and fifth centuries BC. Among their most famous tragedies are *Antigone*, *Oedipus Rex*, *Medea*, and *The Trojan Women*. These plays were typically staged in outdoor theaters, the largest of which was built next to the Acropolis in Athens. It could accommodate an audience of 15,000 spectators. The Greeks were dedicated fans—if they did not enjoy the play, they booed the actors off the stage. If they enjoyed the play, it was not unusual for them to lose themselves completely in the story, sobbing during the most tragic scenes—such as when Oedipus gouges out his own eyes when he learns that he has unwittingly killed his father and married his mother. The Greek playwrights also wrote comedy. In Aristophanes's play *Lysistrata*, written in 411 BC, the women of Greece force their warring city-states to declare peace by withholding sex from their husbands.

Advances in Astronomy

As Greek dramatists, artists, artisans, and architects churned out impressive achievements, other Greeks were making discoveries that would provide the basis on which modern science is built. For example, the Greeks were responsible for some of the earliest discoveries in astronomy. Greek astronomer Anaxagoras, who lived from about 500 BC to 428 BC, correctly deduced that the moon shines by reflecting sunlight. He also suggested that all heavenly bodies are made of the same material as the earth. Anaxagoras did get some things wrong—he thought the sun was a big hot rock and that the Earth is flat.

Another astronomer, Democritus—who lived from about 460 BC to 370 BC—suggested the Milky Way is composed of a great mass of stars. In 585 BC the astronomer and mathematician Thales predicted a solar eclipse based on his study of the motions of the sun and moon. Thales got some things wrong, too. He believed the earth was a floating disk that sat atop a great body of water. The philosopher Xenophanes, who lived from about 570 BC to 478 BC, may have come closest to defining the earth as a planet floating in space when he declared the earth is "rooted in the infinite."[28]

These Greek astronomers made their discoveries without the use of even rudimentary instruments. Not until 1608—some 2,000 years after the era of the ancient Greek astronomers—would a telescope be fashioned by Dutch lens makers and used to make observations of the stars and planets.

Geometry in Ancient Greece

Lacking telescopes, the Greeks were able to make many of their astronomical observations through the use of mathematics, particularly geometry. As the sun, stars, and planets passed overhead, the Greek astronomers envisioned angles to help them measure the motions of heavenly bodies.

The Greek mathematician Euclid, who was born around 300 BC, is regarded as the father of geometry. Euclid's book *The Elements of Geometry* provided answers to geometric problems in the form of postulates. The simplest of Euclid's postulates states that a straight line could be drawn from any point to any other point. He also postulated that a circle has a center and a diameter, which is a straight line that extends through the center of the circle. He also postulated that all 90-degree angles, also known as right angles, are equal.

An earlier Greek mathematician, Pythagoras, who was born around 582 BC and died around 500 BC, helped lay the groundwork for Euclidean geometry when he devised the Pythagorean theorem. That theorem states that in a triangle with a 90-degree angle, if all three sides serve as the sides of square boxes, the area of the square of the side opposite the right angle, known as the hypotenuse, would be equal to the sum of the areas of the squares of the other two sides. Moreover, Pythagoras expressed the theorem in a mathematical equation: $a^2 + b^2 = c^2$. The Pythagorean theorem is a simple equation, but it helped establish the notion that all things in the universe could be explained through mathematics.

Advancements in Medicine

For centuries the Greeks as well as other peoples of the ancient world understood little about the human body or its common ailments. An ill person was believed to be suffering the wrath of the gods. A "physician" of the era was likely to administer home-brewed potions to alleviate the suffering of the patient; the effectiveness of these potions was questionable at best. Moreover, family members were encouraged to appeal to Panacea—the Greek goddess of healing—to rid the patient of his or her illness. Today, the term "panacea" is used to describe a remedy for all ills—an impossibility, of course, just as an appeal to the goddess Panacea was unlikely to heal the ill relative.

The Greek physician Hippocrates, who lived from about 450 BC to 380 BC, revolutionized medicine, turning it into a science based on the understanding that diseases are caused by natural circumstances and not punishments inflicted by the gods. Hippocrates believed poor diets were at the root of many illnesses, and he counseled his patients to exercise and dress warmly during cold weather. He determined that some diseases are infectious—meaning they can be passed from person to person—long before the nineteenth-century chemist Louis Pasteur discovered that diseases are spread by germs. Hippocrates also counseled his patients to see him as soon as they noticed symptoms, believing that diseases are best treated in their earliest stages. Many of Hippocrates's theories have stood the test of time and are part of the practice of medicine today.

Birth of Greek Philosophy

The base on which all Greek mathematics, science, and the arts are built is philosophy—the marketplace of ideas that guided the artists and scientists as they pursued knowledge. Many Greek philosophers attempted to explain the nature of things, but the work of three stands out above the rest: Socrates, Plato, and Aristotle.

Born in 470 BC, Socrates was originally a sculptor and later served Athens as a soldier, distinguishing himself for his bravery in several battles. As he grew older he spent much of his time in the Athenian markets and other public places, talking to citizens and engaging them in dialogue on whatever happened to be on his mind. He was the first philosopher to urge people to engage in self-examination, to question their own opinions as well as those of others. Throughout his life he wrote down little, but he believed all vice was a result of ignorance and that to seek knowledge is a virtue. He believed the pursuit of knowledge should be a lifelong goal.

Although Socrates held no formal classes, students sought him out to gain his wisdom. One of his closest followers was Plato. Born in 428 BC, Plato was a member of an aristocratic family. Unlike Socrates, Plato established a school—the Academy—in Athens. Considered the first European university, students took classes in science, mathematics, politics, and philosophy. Also unlike Socrates, Plato wrote down his thoughts in the form of what are known as "dialogues." Among these dialogues is the *Republic*, in which Plato draws a line between what could be regarded as opinion and what must be considered actual knowledge. According to Plato, the highest level of awareness is actual knowledge because it is founded on reason. When properly used, Plato argues, reason results in valuable insights. The *Republic* also discusses the "myth of the cave," in which Plato argues that those without knowledge are like people shackled together in a dark cave, and only by breaking their shackles can they escape into the sunlight to see things as they truly are.

The Pursuit of Virtue

One of the students at the Academy in Athens was Aristotle. Born in 384 BC, Aristotle was the son of a physician. He arrived at Plato's school at the age of 17 and remained there for 20 years, first as a student and then as a teacher. Later, he worked as a private tutor to the sons of aristocrats and rulers including Alexander the Great.

Aristotle lectured his students on a number of topics, including natural science, astronomy, and biology. He devoted many of his lectures to the study of ethics and his belief that all individuals are motivated by the pursuit of happiness. He examined virtue, which he found to be a form of human excellence, and determined there are two types of virtue: moral and intellectual.

During his many lectures, the Greek philosopher Aristotle examined the topics of ethics, virtue, and happiness. He believed that all individuals are motivated by the pursuit of happiness.

To attain moral virtue, Aristotle argued, people must be constantly making decisions to accept the proper course through life. The display of courage, for example, is a moral virtue, but it can only be reached if a person is able to conquer cowardice while avoiding irrational bravado. Intellectual virtues, he argued, are reached in the pursuit of knowledge in the sciences and the arts, which includes the crafts because Aristotle believed that learning to make ordinary household implements such as urns could be regarded as the pursuit of knowledge. The pursuit of philosophy was also an intellectual virtue, Aristotle believed, because it is a combination of reason and science.

As the work of Aristotle, Plato, and Socrates illustrates, the ancient Greek world was about much more than a constant state of warfare. Under the Greek philosophers, people started questioning their roles in life. Moreover, the Greek astronomers, physicians, and mathematicians were among the first to suggest that the gods did not have total control over the lives of mortals—that there were also natural explanations behind the mysteries of life.

Chapter 4

The Decline and Fall of Ancient Greece

For the Greeks, winning two wars against the Persians was a tremendous achievement. The Greeks were outnumbered in both campaigns; moreover, the city-states, particularly Athens and Sparta, had always been uneasy allies. The Greeks won their two wars against the Persians despite being highly suspicious of one another and hardly willing to cooperate in battle.

In 478 BC the city-states of Greece—fearing yet another war with Persia—formed a voluntary alliance known as the Delian League, so named because the league was established on the Greek island of Delos. Finally putting their long-held animosities aside, the city-states agreed to pool their treasuries and combine their armies to defend Greece against future invasions by Persia. At first the league members cooperated and drove Persian occupiers out of Greek settlements along the Aegean Sea's Turkish coast as well as from Thrace—a region that today is part of Bulgaria and Turkey.

Over the next five decades the Delian League fulfilled its mission: It protected Greece from Persian aggression. Over this time, however, Athens grew in prosperity and became the dominant member of the Delian League—even overseeing the treasury, which by now had grown quite large. Indeed, the other members of the Delian League had cause for concern. Athens had used its wealth and powerful navy to exert authority over trade in the Aegean Sea. "Athens allowed free trade there in time of peace [but] no vessel might sail the sea without her consent," says Will Durant. "Athenian agents decided the destination of every vessel that left the grain ports."[29]

Once again the city-states fell into their old habits of mistrust and envy. They suspected that Athenian officials were looting the Delian League treasury. In 431 BC an incident touched off a conflict that would eventually cause Athens and the entire country to suffer grave consequences. Corcyra, an island colony under the rule of Corinth, declared its independence. As a sea battle raged between Corinth and Corcyra, the Athenians came to the aid of Corcyra. When Athens took the side of the rebels, the Spartans rallied to aid their longtime allies, the Corinthians. The war escalated into a conflict between Athens and Sparta. Eventually, this conflict—known as the Peloponnesian War—would spark the decline and fall of ancient Greece.

Ill-Advised Strategy

The Athenian historian Thucydides recorded many attempts between the Spartan and Athenian leaders to resolve their differences through diplomacy. But the original purpose of the alliance between the two bitter foes—a common defense against the Persians—had long since passed from the memories of their current leaders. Said Thucydides, "The Peloponnesus and Athens were both full of young men whose inexperience made them eager to take up arms."[30]

Soon, the entire country was caught up in the civil war. City-states took sides. Sparta won the allegiance of every city-state in Peloponnesus except Argos, its longtime enemy. Most of the island states in the Aegean Sea backed Athens.

Pericles, the leader of Athens, concocted an ill-advised strategy to win the war. Knowing that Sparta possessed the better infantry, Pericles knew his troops would never defeat the Spartans on the battlefield. And so he ordered all Athenians to remain behind the city's walls. Moreover, he summoned all the citizens of Attica to take refuge within the Athenian walls as well. He refused to send his troops into battle. He planned to use the Athenian navy, which was far superior to the Spartan navy, to wage the war.

During the Peloponnesian War, Athenian triremes (pictured in this eighteenth-century print) battered Spartan boats along the coastline. The war between Athens and Sparta—sometime allies but more often foes—contributed to the downfall of ancient Greece.

At first the strategy was effective. The Athenian triremes constantly battered the smaller Spartan boats along the Peloponnesian coastline. But a year into the war the Athenians ran into some bad luck. Unable to tend their farms outside the city walls, Athens was running short of food. Plague found its way into the city as well. Disease killed a fourth of the Athenian soldiers and took a heavy toll on the civilian population as well—perhaps killing as much as a third of the city's population. In his history of the Peloponnesian War, Thucydides describes the symptoms:

> People in good health were all of a sudden attacked by violent heats in the head, and redness and inflammation in the eyes, the inward parts, such as the throat or tongue, becoming bloody and emitting an unnatural and fetid breath. These symptoms were followed by sneezing and hoarseness, after which the pain soon reached the chest, and produced a hard cough. When it fixed in the stomach, it upset it; and discharges of bile of every kind named by physicians ensued, accompanied by very great distress. In most cases, also an ineffectual retching followed, producing violent spasms which in some cases ceased soon after, in others much later.[31]

Physicians were powerless to treat the victims. In fact, according to Thucydides most Athenian physicians were reluctant to examine or treat the victims for fear that they would contract the plague themselves. In the early months of the disease many physicians died after they contracted the plague.

Socrates Stands Alone

Frightened and ill, many of the Athenians demanded that Pericles be deposed. He was driven from office and soon died of the plague himself. Over the next several years, Athens would be ruled by a series of ill-advised and rash archons, all seeking ways to end the war while maintaining Athenian authority over Sparta. The immediate successor to Pericles was Cleon, a devious Athenian politician who ascended to the post of archon in 429 BC. His most notorious act was the order for all adult males of Mytilene, a town on the island of Lesbos, to be put to death when the Mytilene citizens declared they could not continue to support Athens in the war. A ship of Athenian soldiers was actually dispatched to carry out the edict, but the Athenian Assembly—coming to its senses—dispatched a second ship to Mytilene, arriving at the island just in time to prevent the massacre.

The recall of the death sentence on the male population of Mytilene was one of the few times the Athenian Assembly defied the city-state's ruler. In most other cases, the assembly members agreed to support the bad decisions and faulty military strategies devised by the aristocratic leaders of Athens, who, as the war progressed, were becoming more and more autocratic. Says Victor Davis Hanson, "No government was as reckless and dangerous as Athens' assembly, composed of many leaders who had traveled the Aegean. Yet the [assembly] in a minute's fit could call for the execution of a man—or an entire captured city across the seas—on the flimsiest of charges."[32]

The one Athenian who called for reason and logic was Socrates, who often rose during meetings of the assembly to question the conduct of the war. Socrates had occasionally joined the Athenian soldiers in battle, but in the assembly he raised many uncomfortable questions about the purpose of the war. For Socrates, his arguments were simply in keeping with his philosophy of life—to always be introspective and raise questions and doubts about all decisions. For a city-state fighting a war, the questions posed by Socrates were often regarded as treasonous.

A typical example occurred following the naval battle of Arginusae, just east of Lesbos, in 406 BC. The battle resulted in an Athenian victory—but at a grave cost. As the battle ended, a huge storm swept through the region. During the storm many of the Athenian ships sank, and their crews were forced to jump overboard. Hundreds of Athenian sailors bobbed in the choppy waters, waiting to be rescued. But the storm made that impossible; fearing they would capsize in the rough waters, the surviving vessels were forced to flee. The Athenian sailors who were struggling for their lives in the rough Aegean waters all drowned—many losing their lives within sight of the survivors.

Back in Athens, six admirals were brought to trial, charged with ignoring the fate of the doomed sailors. The assembly voted to execute the admirals. Socrates rose from his seat in the assembly and defended the admirals, offering the lone voice of dissent. The verdict of the assembly was carried out, and many members of the crowd expressed anger at Socrates and vowed that he would one day regret his defense of the admirals.

Slaughter at Aegospotamoi

Meanwhile, the war was going badly for Athens. Turmoil dominated the city. Most of the male population was absent, drafted into the Athenian army and navy or left for dead on the battlefields of Greece. "Back in Athens, panic joined gossip in the lanes and courtyards, in the agora and the assembly," says Bettany Hughes, historian for King's College in London, England. "The flower of the city, the Athenian youth, was abroad. . . . The early toleration of the democratic state was forgotten. Citizens were tortured and executed."[33]

In 413 BC, a two-year campaign on the island of Sicily ended in an Athenian defeat—all Athenian soldiers were killed in battle, executed by their captors, or made into slaves. Moreover, during the course of the war, the best Athenian military leaders had either been killed in battle or exiled after disputes with the assembly or archons. By now, Athens suffered from a dearth of skilled military leaders. The new leaders of the Athenian military found themselves leading hoplites and trireme crews who were young and green, untested in battle. Above all, they lacked the discipline that is vital for a military to be effective.

In 405 BC a Spartan fleet encountered an Athenian fleet of triremes along the shoreline of Aegospotamoi, located on the Turkish coast. For four days, the Spartan commander Lysander watched the Athenian fleet as its crew members camped lazily on the Aegospotamoi beach. On the fifth day, Lysander struck—ordering his ships to attack the Athenians. Hanson explains what happened next:

> The result was an abject slaughter. The Spartan fleet destroyed, disabled, or captured 170 of 180 triremes, dispersed thousands of the oarsmen, and then executed 3,000 to 4,000 of the captured Athenian crews, sparing only the allies and slaves. . . . This most decisive naval defeat in the history of any Greek city-state was not even really fought at sea, and in a sense was not a battle . . . at all. Rather, Lysander's [ships] surprised thousands as they ate, slept, and lounged on the beach. And nearly all the Athenian ships that managed to leave shore were sunk in the shallow surf.[34]

What Killed the Athenians?

Historians and physicians have attempted for decades to identify the disease that wiped out as much as a third of the population of Athens during the Peloponnesian War. Among the suspected culprits are anthrax, bubonic plague, smallpox, and tuberculosis. Thanks to the science of genetics, scientists believe they now have the answer.

In 2006 scientists exhumed the remains of plague victims from the ancient Kerameikos cemetery in Athens. They were able to extract DNA from the dental pulp found in the teeth of the victims. The genetic makeup of the dental pulp contained the DNA for *Salmonella typhi*, the germ that causes typhoid fever.

Typhoid fever is an infectious disease spread by ingesting water or food contaminated with the fecal matter from carriers. Moreover, the symptoms described by the historian Thucydides closely resemble those of typhoid fever. Given the overcrowded and unsanitary conditions of Athens at the time it was under siege by the Spartans, scientists consider it likely that conditions were ripe for a typhoid epidemic.

Aegospotamoi was the last major battle of the war. In 404 BC Athens surrendered to Sparta—bringing to a close the 27-year Peloponnesian War.

The Spartans imposed autocratic command over the Athenians, briefly ending their democracy by imposing the rule of the Council of Thirty, a group of aristocrats who ruled Athens with an iron fist. The council executed and exiled aristocrats and other leaders and severely limited the power of the assembly. The council's rule lasted less than a year; its members were overthrown by Athenian rebels who restored full democracy to the city-state.

Socrates on Trial

By now, Athens was in shambles. Many of the male citizens of the city-state had been killed in warfare. Its navy devastated by the defeat at Aegospotamoi, just a handful of triremes remained seaworthy. The Athenians could no longer protect their settlements along the Turkish coast. These settlements soon fell victim to Persian attacks.

Athens's new leaders looked for a scapegoat—someone on whom to blame the outcome of the war. They settled on Socrates, who had consistently questioned the war. In 399 BC Socrates was put on trial, convicted of trumped up charges of worshipping false gods and corrupting youth, and sentenced to death—forced to drink the poison hemlock. Plato witnessed his teacher's death. Later, Plato wrote,

> Raising the cup to his lips, quite readily and cheerfully he drank off the poison. And hitherto most of us had been able to control our sorrow; but now when we saw him drinking, and saw too that he had finished the draught, we could no longer forbear, and in spite of myself my own tears were flowing fast; so that I covered my face and wept, not for him, but at the thought of my own calamity in having to part from such a friend. . . .
>
> "What is this strange outcry?" he said. "I sent away the women mainly in order that they might not misbehave in this way, for I have been told that a man should die in peace. Be quiet then, and have patience."
>
> When we heard his words we were ashamed, and refrained our tears; and he walked about until, as he said, his legs began to fail. . . . And he felt [his legs] himself, and said: "When the poison reaches the heart, that will be the end."[35]

As for Athens, its preeminent place among all city-states of Greece had come to an end. Twenty-seven years of warfare had reduced its population, destroyed its army and navy, and drained its treasury.

Continuing Conflicts

The end of the Peloponnesian War did not end the era of civil warfare in Greece. In 395 BC an eight-year conflict known as the Corinthian War broke out between Sparta and her former allies, among them

Downfall of the Council of Thirty

The Council of Thirty, also known as the Thirty Tyrants, was composed of Athenian aristocrats placed in charge of the city-state by the Spartans following the defeat of Athens in the Peloponnesian War. During its rule, the council exiled and executed many aristocrats and others whom it considered threats to its authority. Says historian Will Durant, "[They] exiled five thousand democrats, and put fifteen hundred others to death; they assassinated all Athenians who were distasteful to them politically or personally; they put an end to freedom of teaching, assemblage and speech."

The council had established an oligarchy—a government in which power is reserved in the hands of a few. The council's rule lasted less than a year. In 404 BC an aristocrat in exile, Thrasybulus, mustered an army of some 1,000 loyalists and approached the city. To counter the attack, one of the Tyrants, Critias, attempted to organize a defense but found few Athenians willing to fight. Nevertheless, Critias led a modest force outside the city and met Thrasybulus's soldiers in combat.

Thrasybulus's soldiers won easily. Critias was killed in the combat. Thrasybulus entered the city, ended the rule of the council, and restored democracy to Athens.

Will Durant, *The Story of Civilization, vol. 2: The Life of Greece*. New York: Simon & Schuster, 1966, p. 81.

Thebes and Corinth. Athens, by now free of Spartan rule, came to the assistance of Sparta's enemies.

The war was sparked when Sparta sent its fleet to the Turkish coast to reclaim the Greek settlements seized by Persia during the Peloponnesian War. To rid themselves of the Spartans, the Persians urged Thebes to seize the polis Phocis, a Spartan ally. The strategy worked; the Spartans were forced to return to the Greek mainland to defend Phocis. Once again, though, many of the city-states of Greece—including Sparta and Athens—were at war. The Corinthian War ended after the Battle of Cnidus, just off the Turkish coast, when a Spartan fleet was destroyed by Athenian triremes. Now Sparta was as weak as Athens had been at the conclusion of the Peloponnesian War. In 387 BC Sparta and its enemies signed the Peace of Antalcidas, so named for the Spartan diplomat who negotiated the terms of the treaty.

And yet war in Greece continued. During the decades of the 370s and 360s BC many of the city-states were engaged in almost constant conflict. In the 360s BC Thebes—believing the Spartans had grown weak after many years of warfare—attempted to dominate the Peloponnesian Peninsula. The Theban general Epaminondas attempted to cut off Sparta from its allies, including Corinth and Phlius. The Thebans were eventually defeated at the Battle of Mantinea in 362 BC by a Spartan army bolstered by a number of allies—including Athens (proof that in ancient Greece, even longtime enemies could occasionally ally themselves against a common foe).

The Emergence of Alexander

From this chaos, a new leader of Greece would emerge in 336 BC when Alexander III ascended the throne of Macedonia, an independent nation north of Greece. Before Alexander Macedonia was ruled by Alexander's father, Philip II, who had great respect for the Greeks and urged his subjects to adopt Greek architecture, science, art, and other facets of Hellenic culture. He was also very mindful of the chaos that dominated the country to the south. After ascending to the throne in 359 BC,

Philip annexed several Greek colonies located along the Macedonian border and in Thrace as well.

In 338 BC Philip defeated an army of Athenians and Thebans at Chaeronea in central Greece. Following his victory at Chaeronea, Philip summoned diplomats from all Greek city-states and forced them to declare him leader of all Greek armies. Philip intended to use the forces under him to launch an attack on Persia, but in 336 BC, before the combined Macedonian-Greek army sailed for Persia, Philip

At the height of his empire, Alexander the Great (pictured on a coin from about 336 BC) ruled over an area that stretched from Macedonia and Greece to Egypt and portions of India, Kyrgyzstan, and Tajikistan. Alexander's many military victories established his reputation as a brilliant military strategist.

was assassinated. His 20-year-old son, Alexander III, succeeded his father as ruler of Macedonia.

Like his father, Alexander admired Greek culture and was well-schooled in Greek literature, science, and art. (As a young boy, Alexander had been tutored by Aristotle.) Later to be known as Alexander the Great, the new ruler quickly consolidated his power, executed his enemies and, in a conference in Corinth, was picked by leaders of the Greek city-states to lead the Greek-Macedonian confederation against the Persians. Over the next several years, Alexander put down rebellions in Thrace, Illyria, and Thebes. In 334 BC he attacked Persia with an army of some 35,000 Macedonian and Greek soldiers, winning a victory at the Granicus River in Turkey and, a year later, defeating Persia again at the Battle of Issus in what is today Syria. As these victories prove, Alexander was the most brilliant military strategist of the era.

A New Empire

At the height of Alexander's rule, the empire he forged stretched from Macedonia and Greece in the west to Egypt in the south to portions of India, Kyrgyzstan, and Tajikistan in the east. It would be a short-lived empire, though. Alexander died while campaigning in Babylon in 323 BC—possibly by poisoning. Soon after his death, the lands he conquered fragmented into individual kingdoms.

As Macedonia's authority over Greece receded, to the west of Greece a new empire was rising—that of the Romans. Macedonia was defeated by Rome in 197 BC. In 149 BC Rome waged war against the city-states of Greece, winning quick victories. By 146 BC Greece was under the complete authority of the Romans. It would remain so until the disintegration of the Roman Empire some 500 years later.

For much of their existence, the ancient Greeks were surrounded by their enemies: Persia to the east and, later, Macedonia to the north and Rome to the west. With their Spartan warriors, Athenian triremes, and brilliance in strategy and tactics, the Greeks likely could have staved off these threats and remained an independent nation. But throughout their history, the Greek city-states refused to unite under a single authority. Moreover, they distrusted one another—a situation that led to one of the most devastating civil wars in world history. The Peloponnesian War weakened the Greek city-states to such a degree that they never recovered, making them easy targets for future conquerors.

Chapter 5

What Is the Legacy of Ancient Greece?

The first modern Olympic Games were held in Athens in 1896. Just 13 countries sent athletes. A highlight of the games was the marathon, a long-distance race covering some 26 miles. The event was named to commemorate the grueling treks undertaken by the messenger Pheidippides at the Battle of Marathon 2,400 years earlier—first to summon the Spartans to the battle and then to announce victory to the Athenians. The first modern marathon was won by a Greek athlete, Spyridon Louis. He instantly became a national hero.

The Olympics have grown into a huge international event that occurs every two years (for decades the Summer Olympics and Winter Olympics were held every four years in the same year, but in 1992 the International Olympic Committee, governing body for the games, split the summer and winter competitions, alternating them every two years.) Countries apply for the right to stage the Olympics years in advance. London won the bidding to host the 2012 Summer Games. The Russian city of Sochi won the bidding to host the 2014 Winter Olympics. Thousands of athletes from around the world compete in the games. In 2008 more than 11,000 athletes from some 200 countries participated in the Summer Games in Beijing, China. The athletes representing the countries that compete in the modern Olympics parade into the Olympic stadium during the opening and closing ceremonies in alphabetical order. However, Greece, in recognition as the founder of the Olympics, always leads the parade of nations. Even the time of the year in which the Summer Olympics are staged, usually late summer, pays tribute to the ancient games, held during a time of year when farmers could attend the events between harvests.

Also, as the city-states of ancient Greece put their differences aside to send their athletes to the Olympic Games of their era, that tradition has been followed in modern times as well. Athletes from North Korea and South Korea—their governments enemies since the partition of the country in the 1940s—marched together as a united Korea during the ceremonies that opened and closed the Olympic Games staged in 2000 and 2004.

Jamaican runner Asafa Powell (in front, in yellow) leads his team to a gold medal in the 4 x 100-meter relay during the 2008 Summer Olympics in Beijing, China. The modern Olympic Games build on a tradition that began in ancient Greece.

But just as the city-states of ancient Greece often fell back into suspicion and hatred for one another, the two Koreas suffered that fate in 2008. That year the two teams refused to march as one nation during the Olympic ceremonies. "Unfortunately, the political powers—both in the South and the North—did not agree and I regret this very much because this is a setback for peace and harmony and reunification,"[36] said Jacques Rogge, president of the International Olympic Committee.

The Fates of Athens and Sparta

The two most powerful city-states of ancient Greece faced vastly different fates over the course of time. After the fall of ancient Greece, Athens remained a vibrant and populated city and the center of art and culture in the country. Today, Athens is the capital of Greece with a population of 3.2 million. Many ancient Greek relics can still be found in Athens, including the remains of the Parthenon atop the Acropolis.

Sparta has not survived as a major city of Greece. All that remains of the ancient kingdom are some ruins near the small modern Greek city of Sparta, which has a population of about 15,000. The most prominent of the ruins are stones from the foundation of the Menelaion, a monument to the Spartan king Menelaus, husband of Helen.

Even Thucydides predicted that Sparta would not survive as a major city. In his history of the Peloponnesian War, he writes, "I suppose that if [Sparta] were to become desolate, and the temples and the foundations of the public buildings were left, that as time went on there would be a strong disposition with posterity to refuse to accept her fame as a true exponent of her power."

Quoted in Thucydides, *The Peloponnesian War by Thucydides*, trans., John H. Finley Jr., New York: Modern Library, 1951, p. 8.

Survival of Ancient Greek Culture

Nevertheless, the modern Olympics illustrate how the customs and culture of ancient Greece have survived over the centuries, remaining an influence on modern life. Just as the finest athletes of Greece gathered every four years to compete in a series of games, the world's best athletes of the modern era participate in the Olympics. Just as those ancient athletes expected no reward for their participation—their only prizes for winning their events were wreaths of laurel leaves—there is no substantial reward for winning modern Olympic events. The winners receive gold medals.

And just as politics, diplomacy, and suspicion often influenced the relations between the city-states of ancient Greece, that state of affairs is certainly true today in the relations among modern nations. Says Will Durant, "Greek civilization is alive; it moves in every breath of mind that we breathe; so much of it remains that none of us in one lifetime could absorb it all. We know its defects—its insane and pitiless wars . . . its tragic failure to unite liberty with order and peace. But those who cherish freedom, reason and beauty will not linger over these blemishes."[37]

Indeed, even before the decline and fall of the ancient Greeks, their influence on the rest of the world was widespread. The Romans also adopted the Athenian principles of democracy. Virtually at the same time that Cleisthenes established the Athenian Assembly, a rebellion swept through Rome ousting what was known as the Etruscan monarchy. Following the ouster of the Etruscan kings (who ruled from a region in northern Italy now known as Tuscany) the Romans established the first representative republic. Instead of permitting citizens a direct vote in the administration of their government, as the Athenians allowed, the Roman republic provided for the election of a senate as well as lesser assemblies.

The establishment of democracy would survive for centuries and become the principles on which the US Constitution is based. In fact, the primary author of the US Constitution and future president, James Madison, gave thought to adopting the Athenian model for the new American democracy but decided against it. He believed a form of government in which every citizen would have a direct say in drafting new laws would prove too unstable. He worried that American versions of Socrates would emerge, causing too much dissent in the assembly. Wrote Madison, "Had every Athenian citizen been a Socrates every Athenian Assembly would still have been a mob."[38] Instead, Madison and the other founders based the new government on the Roman model, providing for elected representatives to meet in Congress for the creation of laws.

Guarantee of Free Speech

Still, the basic principle of Athenian democracy—that every citizen should have a voice in the government—has been maintained by every nation that has adopted democracy as its system of government. Even in feudal Europe, where the landed gentry ruled with complete authority, some democratic principles were observed. To settle disputes, feudal lords often presided over trials in which adversaries and their witnesses would tell their sides of the story. This early form of jurisprudence would form the basis of the modern system of justice—a basic tenet of democracy very much in concert with the Athenian model. Indeed, even Socrates was allowed to speak in his own defense.

In 1215 the English adopted the Magna Carta, limiting the rights of the royalty and, therefore, expanding the rights of the citizens by establishing a parliament. In 1689 the English Parliament adopted a Bill of Rights, guaranteeing free speech—another basic principle developed in Athens. In the Athenian Assembly, every citizen had the right to rise from his seat and speak his mind. The American Bill of Rights also includes a guarantee of free speech in the First Amendment.

But the Greek system was not perfect. The failure of the Greeks to unite their country and, instead, maintain a system of autonomous city-states certainly contributed to the collapse of ancient Greece. Perhaps one of the saddest legacies of ancient Greece is the concept that disputes could be settled through civil war. Since the Peloponnesian War, dozens of countries on virtually all continents on earth have suffered through civil wars. In ancient Greece, the near-constant state of civil war among the city-states weakened them and made them vulnerable to the Roman invasions that commenced in 149 BC.

Today, the city-state is considered an archaic form of government, and just a handful remain. They include Monaco, a tiny principality on the Mediterranean coast known mostly as a resort community for the wealthy and as host for an annual Grand Prix auto race. About 30,000 people live in Monaco in an area of about 1.25 square miles (3 sq. km).

Another city-state is the Asian island nation of Singapore, which has emerged as a financial capital of the Asian world because many

America's founders take part in the formal signing of the US Constitution in 1787. The basic principle of Athenian democracy—that every citizen should have a voice in government—is evident in the United States and other nations around the world.

large Asian banks have established their headquarters there. The city-state covers an area of about 433 square miles (1,121 sq. km) and includes a population of some 4.7 million people. Finally, the city-state Vatican City is located within the borders of Rome but is completely autonomous of the national Italian government or local Roman city government. The Vatican serves as headquarters of the Roman Catholic Church and is under the authority of the pope. There are about 1,000 permanent citizens of Vatican City, which covers about 110 acres (44ha).

A Common Nationalism

Even as Rome dominated the Greeks, the Romans valued the importance the Greeks had placed on education and philosophy. It was typical for Roman aristocrats to send their sons to Greece to study before returning to Rome to take their places managing the family's estate or as members of the Roman senate. In fact, some of Rome's most important leaders studied in Greece as young men—among them Augustus, who became Rome's first emperor.

Rome's domination over the Greeks ended in the fifth century AD with the collapse of its own empire. In AD 410, barbarians known as the Visigoths sacked Rome, easily overpowering a Roman army too weak to defend the city. Greece soon fell under the rule of the Byzantine Empire, the capital of which was Constantinople in Turkey (today, the city is known as Istanbul).

Constantinople maintained authority over Greece until 1204, when the city fell during the Crusades—the wars in which Christian soldiers attempted to exert sovereignty over the holy lands of the Middle East. With the fall of Constantinople, Greece was split into a number of feudal fiefdoms, the largest of which was the Duchy of Athens. Rarely, though, were the Athenians ruled by Greeks. Over the centuries, French, Spanish, and Italian rulers exerted their authority over the Athenians and other Greek peoples. By the fifteenth century, the Ottoman Empire, based in Constantinople, had grown into one of the most powerful kingdoms on earth. The Ottomans

American Schools: Home of the Spartans

Inspired by the fighting spirit of the ancient Greek warriors, at least 10 American colleges and numerous high schools have adopted "Spartans" as the nickname for their athletic teams. The most renowned is Michigan State University, a perennial powerhouse in college football, and basketball.

Michigan State was formerly known as Michigan Agricultural College, and its teams used the nickname "Aggies." In 1925 the school broadened its curriculum beyond farm sciences and took the new name Michigan State College. The school conducted a contest to pick a new nickname for its athletic teams, and somebody submitted the name "Spartans."

The school official who conducted the contest forgot to make note of who submitted the winning entry, so no one has ever been given credit for submitting the nickname. The entries were turned over to George Alderton, sports editor at the *Lansing State Journal*, and he picked the name. "Happily for the experiment, the name took," Alderton said. "It began appearing in other newspapers and when the student publication used it, that clinched it." In 1945 a nine-foot statue (2.7m) of a Spartan soldier was erected on campus.

Other colleges that have adopted the Spartan name for their teams are Case Western Reserve University, Ohio; Norfolk State University, Virginia; Castleton State College, Vermont; D'Youville College, New York; Manchester College, Indiana; San Jose State University, California; and the University of Tampa, Florida, as well as South Carolina Upstate University and University of North Carolina–Greensboro.

Quoted in Spartan Athletics, "The Nickname," 2011. www.msuspartans.com.

spread their empire west, dominating Greece and nearby European countries. Greece remained under Ottoman control until the nineteenth century.

The Return of Democracy

During the early years of the nineteenth century, revolutionary fervor spread through Greece as the country attempted to free itself of Ottoman rule. Peoples who had never been united since the days of the Dorian invasion now shared a common nationalism. The Ottomans were a powerful foe, though, and many rebellious attempts were easily thwarted by the Ottoman army. Finally, in 1827 Great Britain, France, and Russia intervened—sending military aid to the Greek rebels. These nations realized the strategic importance of establishing naval bases in Greece, where they could control commerce in the Mediterranean Sea. In 1829 the Ottomans withdrew from Greece, and a year later France, Great Britain, and Russia declared the London Protocol. This agreement established Greece as an independent kingdom—but with a representative parliament. For the first time since the days of the Athenian Assembly, a form of democracy had returned to Greece.

As with the rest of Europe, though, Greece spent much of the nineteenth century and early years of the twentieth century struggling with popular demands for democracy, the declining powers of monarchs, socialist and anarchist movements, and the animosity many ethnic groups held for one another that finally culminated in 1914 with the outbreak of World War I. Greece's King Constantine I attempted to remain neutral, but in 1917 the monarch gave in to pro-Western pressure in his government, and the country joined the conflict on the side of the Allies.

Following the war a series of military dictators dominated Greece. As fervor for rebellion began to rise again, the dictator General Georgios Kondylis agreed to free elections. In 1928 the Labor Party was elected to a majority of seats in parliament, and Eleutherios Venizelos, one of Greece's most popular politicians, took office as prime minister, returning democracy to the land of its birth.

The Birth of Phi Beta Kappa

Over the centuries, as Greece struggled to regain its independence, other countries recognized the value of the advances in science and art made during the era of the ancient Greeks. In 1511 the Italian painter Raphael completed *The School of Athens*, a fresco on an interior wall of the Apostolic Palace in the Vatican in Rome. The painting depicts Plato and Aristotle as well as major figures in ancient Greek science and mathematics, including Euclid and Pythagoras. In 1819 the English romantic poet John Keats recognized the beauty of ancient Greek ceramics with his poem "Ode on a Grecian Urn."

Ancient Greek influence found its way into the American colonies in the 1770s. In 1776, at the College of William and Mary in Williamsburg, Virginia, many students agitated for independence from England. Talk of revolution was discouraged on campus, so some students reserved their revolutionary rhetoric for the nearby Raleigh Tavern and specifically the tavern's Apollo Room—named after a son of Zeus. During one meeting in the Apollo Room, five students resolved to form a secret society in which they could discuss matters considered too controversial for public dialogue. To name their society, they chose three letters of the Greek alphabet: Phi Beta Kappa.

Soon, branches of Phi Beta Kappa spread to other college campuses in America. Although originally hotbeds of revolutionary dialogue, following the War of Independence the Phi Beta Kappa societies focused on scholarship and social functions. Today, Phi Beta Kappa is a national organization whose members represent the top liberal arts students on American college campuses.

As Phi Beta Kappa grew, so did other campus groups that also wished to be identified by letters of the Greek alphabet. These became college fraternities, and today they can be found on the campuses of most American colleges. The first sorority—an organization for female students—was Pi Beta Phi, founded in 1851 on the campus of Wesleyan Female College in Macon, Georgia.

Contributions to Literature and Language

As the fraternities and sororities of the modern age illustrate, the ancient Greek alphabet remains alive in the twenty-first century. Indeed, many common English words can find their roots in the language of the ancient Greeks. The term "thespian" is often used to describe an actor; Thespis was an important contributor to early Greek drama, adding a spoken prologue to begin the play's performance. (Thespis is not to be confused with the city-state Thespiae, which aided the Spartans at the Battle of Thermopylae.)

"Herculean" is used to describe a formidable task similar to the labors of Heracles, particularly the cleaning of the stables of Augeus. A "spartan" existence describes life as the Spartans knew it; they enjoyed few earthly pleasures and spent the majority of their time in rigorous training. "Colossal" describes the enormity of an object; the word has its root in the Colossus of Rhodes, a 98-foot-tall statue (30m) erected on the Greek island of Rhodes to honor the sun god Helios. Psychologists talk about the "Oedipus complex," the subconscious desire of some sons to marry their mothers—the term is named for the title character of the play by Sophocles, *Oedipus the King*.

In sports, athletes risk ruptures of their Achilles tendons, a major injury that can put them out of action for a season or more. The tendon starts at the heel and reaches up the back of the leg to the calf muscle. It is named for the one vulnerable place on the body of Achilles—his heel—which proved to be his undoing when his enemy Paris killed him by shooting an arrow into his heel.

Legacy of Warfare

For students, ancient Greece remains an important topic of study. The lives and teachings of Socrates, Plato, and Aristotle are studied in high school and college. The Greek tragedies are read by students and con-

A nineteenth-century painting depicts a battle between Greek rebels and the Ottoman army. The Ottomans withdrew from Greece in 1829 only after intervention by European powers. For the first time since the days of the Athenian Assembly, a form of democracy had returned to Greece.

tinue to be performed on stage. In 2011 a new production of the Greek tragedy *Medea* by Euripides opened on the Broadway stage. The play tells the story of the betrayal of the wife of the Greek hero Jason and how she seeks revenge on her husband.

Hollywood films have long mined the rich stories found in Greek myth. Heracles is a familiar character in many Hollywood "sword and sandal" productions. The myth of Jason's search for the golden fleece was told in the big-budget 1963 film *Jason and the Argonauts* that featured some revolutionary special effects. The Greek siege of Troy was depicted in the 2004 film *Troy*, while the heroic stand made by the 300 Spartans at the Battle of Thermopylae has been filmed by Hollywood producers several times, most recently in the 2006 film *300*. In 2011 a number of Greek myths were dramatized in the film *Immortals,* in which Theseus, slayer of the Minotaur, finds new adventures among ancient Greece's mythical heroes and gods.

Some 2,500 years after the Peloponnesian War led to the decline and fall of ancient Greece, the culture of the Greeks remains very much a part of the modern world. Ancient Greece gave the world democracy, theatrical drama, medicine, geometry, philosophy, and the study of the stars and planets. But ancient Greece also left a legacy of warfare. Today's students may find themselves wondering how much more the ancient Greeks could have accomplished had they not devoted so much of their attention and resources to murderous conflict.

Source Notes

Introduction: The Defining Characteristics of Ancient Greece

1. Michael Grant, *The Rise of the Greeks*. New York: Charles Scribner's Sons, 1987, p. xi.
2. Will Durant, *The Story of Civilization,* vol. 2: *The Life of Greece*. New York: Simon and Schuster, 1966, p. 81.
3. Colette Hemingway, "Women in Classical Greece," Metropolitan Museum of Art, 2011. www.metmuseum.org.
4. Quoted in Vincent Gabrielsen, "Warfare and the State," in Philip A.G. Sabin, Hans Van Wees, and Michael Whitby, eds., *The Cambridge History of Greek and Roman Warfare*. New York: Cambridge University Press, 2007, p. 287.
5. Durant, *The Story of Civilization,* vol. 2, p. 27.

Chapter One: What Conditions Led to the Rise of Ancient Greece?

6. Durant, *The Story of Civilization,* vol. 2, p. 63.
7. Quoted in Durant, *The Story of Civilization,* vol. 2, p. 5.
8. Quoted in Edith Hamilton, *Mythology: Timeless Tales of Gods and Heroes*. New York: Mentor, 1942, p. 181.
9. Quoted in Hamilton, *Mythology*, p. 199.
10. Quoted in Caroline Alexander, "Echoes of the Heroic Age," *National Geographic*, December 1999, p. 74.
11. Grant, *The Rise of the Greeks*, p. 147.
12. Hamilton, *Mythology*, p. 18.
13. Quoted in Hamilton, *Mythology*, pp. 161–62.

Chapter Two: Rise of the City-States

14. Herodotus, *The Histories*, trans. Donald Lateiner and G.C. Macauley. New York: Barnes & Noble, 2004, p. 415.

15. Durant, *The Story of Civilization,* vol. 2, p. 107.
16. Thomas George Tucker, *Life in Ancient Athens*. New York: MacMillan, 1916, pp. 3–4.
17. Tucker, *Life in Ancient Athens*. New York: MacMillan, 1916, p. 3.
18. Durant, *The Story of Civilization,* vol. 2, p. 124.
19. Grant, *The Rise of the Greeks*, p. 53.
20. Durant, *The Story of Civilization,* vol. 2, p. 126.
21. Victor Davis Hanson, *The Wars of the Ancient Greeks*. London: Cassell, 1999, p. 50.
22. William Weir, *50 Battles That Changed the World*. Franklin Lakes, NJ: Career Press, 2004, p. 8.
23. Quoted in Hanson, *The Wars of the Ancient Greeks*, p. 18.

Chapter Three: An Era of Achievement

24. Grant, *The Rise of the Greeks*, pp. 26–27.
25. Durant, *The Story of Civilization,* vol. 2, p. 323.
26. Durant, *The Story of Civilization,* vol. 2, p. 327.
27. Jenifer Neils, "A Classical Icon," introduction to Jenifer Neils, ed., *The Parthenon: From Antiquity to the Present*. New York: Cambridge University Press, 2005, p. 1.
28. Quoted in Arthur Koestler, *The Sleepwalkers*. New York: Grosset and Dunlap, 1973, p. 24.

Chapter Four: The Decline and Fall of Ancient Greece

29. Durant, *The Story of Civilization,* vol. 2, p. 439.
30. Quoted in Durant, *The Story of Civilization,* vol. 2, p. 440.
31. Thucydides, *The Peloponnesian War by Thucydides* trans., John H. Finley Jr., New York: Modern Library, 1951, pp. 110–11.
32. Victor Davis Hanson, *A War like No Other: How the Athenians and Spartans Fought the Peloponnesian War*. New York: Random House, 2005, pp. 236–37.
33. Bettany Hughes, *The Hemlock Cup: Socrates, Athens and the Search for the Good Life*. New York: Knopf, 2010, p. 285.
34. Hanson, *A War like No Other*, p. 283.

35. Quoted in Plato, *Phaedo by Plato* trans., Benjamin Jowett. Fairfield, IA: 1st World Library, 2008, pp. 142–43.

Chapter Five: What Is the Legacy of Ancient Greece?

36. Quoted in Stephen Wilson, "North, South Korea Fail to Broker Joint Olympics March," *New York Sun*, August 7, 2008. www.nysun.com.
37. Durant, *The Story of Civilization,* vol. 2, pp. 670–71.
38. Quoted in Sheldon S. Wolin, "Norm and Form: The Constitutionalizing of Democracy," in J. Peter Euben, John R. Wallach, and Josiah Ober, eds., *Athenian Political Thought and the Reconstruction of American Democracy*. Ithaca, NY: Cornell University Press, 1994, p. 33.

Important People of Ancient Greece

Alexander the Great: Following the Peloponnesian War, the Macedonian ruler united the Greek armies in 336 BC and led them in an invasion of Persia. The empire forged by Alexander stretched from Greece and Macedonia in the west to Egypt in the south and portions of India, Kyrgyzstan, and Tajikistan in the east. Alexander's rule ended in 323 BC.

Aristophanes: One of ancient Greece's most accomplished playwrights, Aristophanes, who lived from 448 to 385 BC, wrote tragedies and comedies. He is the author of *Lysistrata*, the comic story of how women from warring city-states withhold sex from their husbands until they make peace.

Aristotle: A student of Plato, he believed all individuals are motivated by the pursuit of happiness. Aristotle also believed in two types of virtue: moral and intellectual. Those who seek moral virtue must constantly test themselves with the decisions they make in life, while the attainment of intellectual virtue must be a lifelong pursuit.

Cleisthenes: The exiled aristocrat returned to Athens in 508 BC after the dictator Isagoras was overthrown. Named archon of Athens, Cleisthenes initiated the first democracy in history when he created the Athenian Assembly and gave each citizen of Athens a vote in the affairs of the city-state.

Euclid: The fourth-century BC mathematician developed geometry. He conceived a number of postulates, an example of which is a straight line can be drawn from any point to any other point.

Homer: The Greek poet, who lived sometime between the ninth and seventh centuries BC, wrote the *Iliad* and the *Odyssey*; the two epic poems tell the story of the Trojan War and the adventures of the mythical Greek heroes Odysseus and Achilles.

Leonidas: King of Sparta. In 480 BC Leonidas and his troops held off thousands of Persian soldiers at the Battle of Thermopylae for three days. When a traitor showed the Persians a route around a narrow mountain pass, Leonidas's men were surrounded and slaughtered. Leonidas and his 300 Spartan warriors remain folk heroes to the people of Greece.

Pericles: Archon of Athens at the outbreak of the Peloponnesian War, Pericles devised the ill-advised strategy of keeping his army within the city walls. When plague swept through Athens, the disease killed a third of the citizens—including Pericles. He oversaw construction of the Parthenon atop the Acropolis, the most magnificent temple in ancient Greece.

Pheidippides: Given the task of summoning the Spartans to the Battle of Marathon in 490 BC, Pheidippides ran 140 miles (255km) to Sparta in two days. After the Athenians defeated the Persians in the battle, he ran 26 miles (42km) to Athens to announce the victory. The modern Olympic marathon is based on the achievements of Pheidippides.

Plato: Born in 428 BC, Plato was a student of Socrates and established the Academy of Athens—the first university in the European world. Plato is author of a number of "dialogues," including the *Republic*, in which he attempts to define the differences between opinion and knowledge based on reason.

Pythagoras: The mathematician, who lived in the sixth century BC, would help lay the groundwork for Euclid to develop geometry. He is known mostly for Pythagorean theorem, which helped establish the notion that all things in the universe could be explained through mathematics.

Socrates: Born in 470 BC, Socrates was the first Greek philosopher to challenge people to question all ideas—even their own. He believed the pursuit of knowledge is a virtue. He grew unpopular when he questioned the Peloponnesian War. When Athens surrendered to Sparta, Socrates was made a scapegoat. He was convicted and sentenced to death.

Solon: Archon of Athens from 594 BC to 558 BC, Solon was the first ruler to give rights to ordinary Athenians. He canceled debts owed by farmers to wealthy aristocrats and returned farmland to their original owners. He also freed farmers who had been sold into slavery to pay off their debts.

Sophocles: The Greek playwright, who is believed to have lived from 496 to 406 BC, authored many of the tragedies of the ancient Greek theater, including *Oedipus Rex*, the story of a son who murders his father and marries his mother. When Oedipus learns the truth of what he has done, he blinds himself.

Themistocles: Following the first Greco-Persian war in 490 BC, Themistocles realized the importance of establishing a powerful navy to protect Athens. Under his direction, the Athenians developed the trireme, a powerful and swift vessel that provided the city-state with an overwhelming advantage in naval warfare.

For Further Research 

Books

Caroline Alexander, *The War That Killed Achilles: The True Story of Homer's "Iliad" and the Trojan War*. New York: Penguin, 2010.

Richard A. Billows, *Marathon: The Battle That Changed Western Civilization*. New York: Overlook, 2010.

Alfred S. Bradford, *Leonidas and the Kings of Sparta: Mightiest Warriors, Fairest Kingdom*. Santa Barbara, CA: Praeger, 2011.

Ken Dowden and Niall Livingstone, eds., *A Companion to Greek Mythology*. Malden, MA: Blackwell, 2011.

Nancy Evans, *Civic Rites: Democracy and Religion in Ancient Athens*. Berkeley: University of California Press, 2010.

Philip Freeman, *Alexander the Great*. New York: Simon & Schuster, 2011.

Bettany Hughes, *The Hemlock Cup: Socrates, Athens and the Search for the Good Life*. New York: Knopf, 2010.

Paul Johnson, *Socrates: A Man for Our Times*. New York: Viking, 2011.

Jon D. Mikalson, *Ancient Greek Religion*. Malden, MA: Blackwell, 2010.

Websites

Ancient Greece (www.yourdiscovery.com/greece/index.shtml). Maintained by the Discovery Channel, the website provides students with an overview of many facets of ancient Greek life, including mythology, politics of the city-states, the first Olympic Games, Greek language, and the rise of Alexander the Great.

Ancient Olympic Games (www.olympic.org/ancient-olympic-games). Maintained by the International Olympic Committee, the website provides students with a background on the first Olympics, staged in Greece in 776 BC. Students will find descriptions of the events and athletes of the original games and can view a seven-minute video explaining the history of the games.

Creatures of Greek Mythology (http://edweb.sdsu.edu/people/bdodge/scaffold/gg/creature.html). A project of San Diego State University's College of Education, the website provides descriptions of many of the creatures found in Greek mythology, including the Cyclops, Medusa and the Gorgons, and the Sirens.

The Glorious Parthenon (www.pbs.org/wgbh/nova/ancient/glorious-parthenon.html). Companion website to the 2008 PBS *Nova* documentary on the Parthenon, the massive Greek temple erected atop the Acropolis in Athens. The website includes a history of construction of the temple and descriptions of the architecture and art of the building. Students can watch a slide show on efforts to restore the 2,500-year-old temple.

Greek Myth Index (www.mythindex.com/greek-mythology/Names-A.html). The online resource provides identifications for more than 3,700 figures and places in Greek mythology. Such familiar figures as the chief god Zeus can be found on the website as well as many obscure names, such as Zephyrus, the lesser god of the west wind.

The Greeks: Crucible of Civilization (www.pbs.org/empires/thegreeks/htmlver). Companion website to the 1999 three-part PBS documentary *The Greeks: Crucible of Civilization*, the website provides a timeline of important dates in ancient Greek history; biographies of key figures from the era, including Cleisthenes, Pericles, and Socrates; and a background on the Parthenon, including a 3D animation of the ancient temple.

Labors of Hercules (www.perseus.tufts.edu/Herakles/labors.html). Maintained by Tufts University in Massachusetts, the website describes the 12 labors of Hercules (the Latinized name for the Greek hero Heracles). The website describes Heracles's battles with the serpent known as the Hydra, the deadly bull of Crete, the man-eating horses of Thrace, and the hero's cleansing of the stables of Augeas.

Livius.org (www.livius.org/greece.html). Written by Dutch historian Jona Lendering, the website contains dozens of articles describing ancient Greek communities, battles, leaders, and mythical figures. Among the obscure details students will find on the site are descriptions of the terrain at Thermopylae and the height of the Colossus of Rhodes—about 98 feet (30m).

Index

Note: Boldface page numbers indicate illustrations.

Academy, the, 52
Achilles, 19, 78, 22
Aegean Sea, 18, 37, 55, 56
Aegospotamoi, Battle of, 60–61
Aeneas, 20
Aeneid, The (Virgil), 20
Aeschylus, 47, 49
agriculture
goddess of, 23
olives, 42, 43
as part of Greek legacy, 14
reforms of Solon, 35
Aietes (king of Colchis), 25–26
Aigion, 13
Alcmena, 24
Alexander III (the Great), 64, **65**, 66
Anatolia. *See* Trojan War
Anaxagoras, 49
Antalcidas, Peace of, 64
Aphrodite (goddess), 19, 23, 26
Apollo (god), 23
architecture, 46–48, **48**
Ares (god), 23
Arginusae, Battle of, 59
Argo (ship), 25
Argonauts, 25–26
Argos, 37, 56
Ariadne, 28
aristocracy, Athenian, 32, 33, 35–36, 59, 61, 63
Aristophanes, 49
Aristotle, 52–54, **53**, 66
Artemis (goddess), 23
arts
architecture, 46–48, 48
modern appreciation of Greek, 77
painting, 45–46
pottery, 43, 45
sculpture, 45
theater, 47, 49, 78, 79
astronomy, 49–50
Athena (goddess)
Athens and, 34
as Olympian, 23
Perseus and, 28
temples to, 47–48, 48
Athenian government
democratic
development of, 11, 35–37
during Peloponnesian War, 59, 60
restoration of, 61, 63
rule by Council of Thirty, 61, 63
rule by despots and aristocracy, 33
Athens
annexation of city-states by, 37
Battle of Marathon, 38–41
as center of trade and commerce, 32
Corinthian War and, 64
as Delian League member, 55–56
modern, 70
naming of, 34
navy of, 40, 55–57, 57
origins of, 18
Peloponnesian War, 46, 56–63
pottery in, 45
rights of inhabitants of, 11, 12, 31–32, 35–36
war with Crete, 28
athletics
names of American teams, 75
Olympic Games, 44
modern, 68–71, 69
origin of, 42
spirit of, 42–43
of Spartan women, 32
Attica, 18, 32, 56
See also Athens
Augean stables, 17, 78

Battle of Aegospotamoi, 60–61
Battle of Arginusae, 59

Battle of Cnidus, 64
Battle of Mantinea, 64
Battle of Marathon, 38–41
Battle of Salamis, 30
Battle of Thermopylae, 29–30, 31, 40, 79–80
beliefs
of Dorians, 16
in gods and goddesses
depicted in arts, 43
directed actions of humans, 12–13
illness and, 51
lesser, 23–24
Olympians, 23
as source of guidance, 24
temples dedicated to, 46–48, 48
warfare among Greeks and, 28
See also specific deities
myths about heroes, 13
oracles and, 13
black-figure pottery, 45
bravery, importance of, 11, 13
Byzantine Empire, 74

Calliope (Muse), 23
cave, myth of, 52
Cecrops, 34
Chiron (centaur), 25
city-states
adoption of democracy by, 36–37
alliance against Persia, 29–30
alliances among, 55–56
conquest by Rome, 66, 73
cultures of, 31–32
disunity and conquest of, 67
modern, 73–74
Olympic Games and, 42, 43
origins of, 10–11
warfare among, 28, 37, 41, 63–64
See also Athens; Peloponnesian War; Sparta; specific city-states
Cleisthenes
development of democracy, 35, 36–37, 42
overthrow of Hippias, 33
Cleon, 58
Cnidus, Battle of, 64
Colchis, 25–26
commerce, Athens as center of, 32
Constantinople, 74
Corcyra, 56
Corinth
Corinthian War, 63–64
first Dorian city in, 15
pottery, 45
Corinthian War, 63–64
Council of Thirty, 61, 63
Crete
earliest inhabitants, 18
war with Athens, 28
Critias, 63
Cyclades, 18
Cyclops, 26, 28

Darius (king of Persia), 39
debt-bondage system, 35–36
Delian League, 55–56
democracy
continuation of, 71–72
derivation of word, 36
development of, 11, 35–37
importance of Battle of Marathon to, 41
modern, 36–37, 76–77
Olympic Games and, 42–43
restoration of, 61, 63
in Rome, 71, 72
warfare and loss of, 59, 60
Democritus, 49
dialogues of Plato, 52
Discobolos (sculpture), 45
Discus Thrower (sculpture), 45
Dorians, 15–16, 34, 46
Doric columns, 46
Dorus, 15
Durant, Will
on Athenian control of seas, 55–56
on Athenian democracy, 37
on Council of Thirty, 63
on dictatorship of Hippias, 33
on the Discus Thrower, 45
on Dorians, 16
on Greek Chorus, 47
on Greek temples, 46
on legacy of Greek civilization, 14, 71
on naming of Greece, 30
on Spartan army and moral code, 11

Elements of Geometry, The (Euclid), 50
England, 11, 20, 72, 77
Epaminondas, 64
Ephialtes, 29
Erato (Muse), 23
Eros (god), 24

Euclid, 50
Euripides, 49, 79
Eurystheus (king of Mycenae), 17

fraternities, 77–78
free speech, 72

geometry, 50, 80
golden fleece, 25–26
Gorgons, 27, 28
Graces, the (goddesses), 23
Graii, 30
Grant, Michael
on Iliad and Odyssey, 22–23
on importance of ancient Greeks, 10
on pottery, 45
on Solon, 36
Greco-Persian wars
Battle of Marathon, 38–41
Battle of Thermopylae, 29–30, 31
city-state alliances and, 55
Greece
under Byzantine Empire, 74
map of, 38
modern, 70, 76–77
origin of name, 30
under Ottoman Empire, 74, 76, 79
Greek Chorus, 47

Hades, 23
Hamilton, Edith, 24
Hanson, Victor Davis
on hoplite fighting, 39
on Peloponnesian War, 59, 60
on triremes, 40
Harpies, 25
Helen (of Troy), 19, 21, 22, 46
Helios (god), 15, 78
Hellas, derivation of word, 15
Hemingway, Colette, 12
Hera (goddess)
Heracles and, 17, 24–25
Jason and, 25, 26
as Olympian, 23
Heracles
as baby, 24–25
Dorians and, 16
Hera and, 17, 24–25
modern language and, 78
in movies, 79
Olympic Games and, 42
twelve labors of, 17
Heraclitus, 41
Hermes (god), 23
Herodotus, 30
Herse (goddess), 23–24
Hipparchus, 33
Hippias, 33
Hippocrates, 51
Homer, 18–19, 22–23, 24
hoplites, 39–40
Horae (goddesses), 23
Hughes, Bettany, 60

Iliad (Homer), 18–19, 22–23
illness
Athenian plague during Peloponnesian War, 57–58, 61
beliefs about, 51
Iolcus (city-state), 25–26
Iris (goddess), 23
Isagoras, 33–34

Jason, 25–26, 79

Keres (goddesses), 23–24
Koreas and Olympic Games, 69–70
Korfmann, Manfred, 21

Lacedaemon, 34
Lacoön, 20
language, 31, 32, 78
Leda, 15
legacy
Olympic Games, 68–71, 69
as source of Western civilization, 10, 14, 71
warfare, 39, 72–73
See also democracy
Leonidas (king of Sparta), 30, 31
Lesbos, 58–59
London Protocol, 76
Louis, Spyridon, 68
Lysander, 60
Lysistrata (Aristophanes), 49

Macedonia, 64–66
Madison, James, 71–72
Magna Carta, 11, 72
Mantinea, Battle of, 64
Marathon, Battle of, 38–41
marriage, 12, 23

mathematics, 50
Medea and Jason, 26
medicine, 51
Medusa (Gorgon), 27, 28
Melpomene (Muse), 23
Menelaus (king of Sparta), 19, 21, 70
Minos (king of Crete), 28
Minotaur, 28, 80
Monaco, 73
Mount Olympus, 23
movies, 79–80
Muses (goddesses), 23
Mycenae, 17
mythological heroes
  depicted in arts, 43
  importance of, 13
  Jason, 25–26
  in movies, 79–80
  Perseus, 27, 28
  Theseus, 28
  See also Heracles
Mytilene, 58–59

Neils, Jenifer, 48
Neolithic Age, 16, 18

Odysseus
  Cyclops and, 26, 28
  overview of adventures of, 19
  Trojan Horse and, 21
Odyssey (Homer), 18–19, 22–23, 24
Oedipus complex, 78
oligarchy, 63
olives, 42, 43
Olympians, 23, 34
Olympic Games, 44
  modern, 68–71, 69
  origin of, 42
  spirit of, 42–43
oracles, 13, 25, 33–34
Ottoman Empire, 74, 76, 79

painting, 45–46
Panacea (goddess), 51
Paris, 19, 21, 78
Parthenon, 46–48, **48**, 70
Peace of Antalcidas, 64
Peisistratus, 33
Pelias (king of Iolcus), 25
Peloponnesian War
  Athenian strategy, 56–61
  consequences of, 61–63
  disease during, 57–58, 61
  origin of, 46
Peloponnesus, 15–16, 18, 42
Penia (goddess), 24
Pericles
  Parthenon construction, 47
  Peloponnesian War and, 56, 58
Perseus, 27, 28
Persia
  Corinthian War, 64
  Greco-Persian wars
    Battle of Marathon, 38–41
    Battle of Thermopylae, 29–30, 31
    city-state alliances and, 55
  war with Greek-Macedonian
    confederation, 65–66
Pheidippides, 39, 68
Phi Beta Kappa, 77–78
Philip II (king of Macedonia), 64–66
Philoctetes, 21
philosophy, 51–54
Plataea, 37
Plato, 52, 62
poleis. *See* city-states
Polygnotus, 46
Polyphemus (Cyclops), 26, 28
polytheism, 23–24
  See also specific deities
Poros (god), 24
Poseidon (god), 23, 34
pottery, 43, 45
Priam (king of Troy), 19, 21
property, ownership of, 31, 32
Pythagoras, 50

red-figure pottery, 45
religion. *See* beliefs
Republic (Plato), 52
Return of the Heracleidae, 16
Rogge, Jacques, 70
Rome
  adoption of Greek civilization by, 74
  conquest by, 10, 66, 73
  democracy in, 71, 72
  founding of, 20
  name for Greece and, 30

Salamis, Battle of, 30
science, 49–50, 51
sculpture, 45

Selene (goddess), 23
Singapore, 73–74
Sirens (goddesses), 24
slaves/slavery, 12, 15, 35, 37, 60
Socrates, 52, 59, 62
Solon, 35–36
Sophocles, 47, 49
sororities, 77
Sparta
Battle of Marathon, 39–41
Battle of Thermopylae, 29–30, 31
Corinthian War, 63–64
founding of, 34
Isagoras's rule of Athens and, 33–34
males in, 11, 30
modern, 70
moral code of, 11
in movies, 79–80
names of American athletic teams, 75
origin of, 16
Peloponnesian War, 46, 56–63
war with Argos, 37
women in, 12, 31, 32
spiritual beliefs. *See* beliefs
Sybaris, 37

Teiresias, 25
Terpsichore (Muse), 23
Thales, 49
theater, 47, 49, 78, 79
Thebes, 64, 66
Themistocles, 40
Thermopylae, Battle of, 29–30, 31, 40, 79–80
Theseus, 28, 80
Thetis, 19
Thirty Tyrants, 63
Thrasybulus, 63
Thucydides
on Peloponnesian War, 56, 58
on survival of Sparta, 70
trade
Athens as center of, 32
in olives, 43
as part of Greek legacy, 14
Trojan War and, 21
triremes, 30, 40, 56–57, 57
Trojan Horse, 19–21
Trojan War
in art, 46
conduct of, 18–21, 22
in movies, 79
victory in, 10
Troy (city-state), 21
Tucker, George, 32
typhoid fever, 61

United States
athletic teams, 75
Constitution, 71–72, 73
fraternities and sororities, 77–78
Phi Beta Kappa, 77–78

Vatican City, 74
Virgil, 20, 21
virtue, 52–54

warfare
among city-states, 28, 37, 41, 63–64
depicted in arts, 43, 46
goddesses of warriors in death, 23
Greco-Persian wars, 29–30, 31, 38–41, 55
Greek-Macedonian confederation, 65–66
Greek strategy, 39–40
importance of, 10, 11
iron weapons and, 15
as legacy of Greek civilization, 39, 72–73
loss of democracy during, 59, 60
naval, 40, 57, 59, 60
Peloponnesian War, 46, 56–63
Spartan way of life and, 11, 30
as tool of gods, 28
Trojan War, 10, 18–21, 22, 46
Weir, William, 41
women
age at marriage, 12
Athenian, 12, 31–32
Spartan, 12, 31, 32
theater and, 47
writing, as part of Greek legacy, 14

Xenophanes, 49–50
Xerxes (king of Persia), 29

Zeus (god)
Heracles and, 16, 17, 24
as Olympian, 23

Picture Credits

Cover: © Leonardo de Selva/Corbis

AP Images: 69

© Bettmann/Corbis: 22, 73

HIP/Art Resource, NY: 44

© Hoberman Collection/Corbis: 65

© Lebrecht/Lebrecht Music & Arts/Corbis: 27

© National Geographic Society/Corbis: 31

© Michael Nicholson/Corbus: 57

© Stapleton Collection/Corbis: 79

Thinkstock/liquidlibrary: 8

Thinkstock/Photos.com: 9 (top right), 53

Thinkstock/iStockphoto: 9 (top left), bottom, 48

Steve Zmina: 38

People in a panathenaic procession bring a new robe to Athena (colour litho), Herget, Herbert M. (1885-1950)/National Geographic Image Collection/The Bridgeman Art Library: 13

About the Author

Hal Marcovitz is a former newspaper reporter and columnist and the author of more than 150 books for young readers. His other title in the Understanding World History series is *Ancient Rome*.